Take Control Retirement Plan

Radon Stancil

Contents

Acknowledgements

I would like to say thank you to my wife, Jenifer, and my two children, Jackson and Bella. Your support and trust have allowed me to have some of the greatest opportunities. Without your help I would not be able to accomplish my goals. My commitment to you is to be focused on the more important things, and to not get sidetracked by everyday affairs that rob me of the wonderful privilege of being with you. I love you very much.

I would also like to thank my mother and father who have always allowed me to try. You never told me I could not do something that I wanted to try. You helped me to focus my goals in the right place. Because of this, I have had many privileges.

I would also like to thank Ronda Swaney for your great help in editing this book. Your talent, thoughts, and insight are greatly appreciated.

rules that apply to us all. For example, how much can you put into an IRA? How much must you withdraw from your IRA starting at age 70 1/2? In this book, I have answered some of these questions to help you understand a few of the basic guidelines. But what is the best way to apply the "common" rules to your family? That is the tricky part!

Each year I do several educational seminars and meet many different people. At one of these seminars a man approached me and began to tell me about his unique situation. He had accumulated a very nice estate. To educate himself, he decided to go to school and take all the courses needed to become a Certified Financial Planner. He did not take the exam and had no desire to practice financial planning. He simply wanted to understand the rules and know the best way to guide his own family. I found his dedication pretty impressive. But the most impressive thing was that even after all the education he had received, he was wise enough to realize the rules are always changing. He knew a lot more than most people, but he still realized that his situation was unique and that he would need ongoing guidance.

I don't want you to feel like you need to become a financial planner to understand your own retirement. My goal is to help you understand some of the rules. At the same time, I want to make sure you know that the rules are always changing and that you must stay aware of those changes. I want to provide you with some guidance, but ensure that you know guidance should be ongoing. I want you to know there is no master product or one-size-fits-all plan. No expert has created a foolproof solution for everyone. Even if you rely on a professional, that does not mean you don't need to be well-educated on the subject of finances or retirement planning. It is fine and even advisable to read articles, attend seminars, make phone calls to advisors, talk to neighbors, and even consider acting on a great tip. By all means, get and stay educated about retirement. But keep proach would mean designing your personal plan. Your retirement plan will undoubtedly need to be different from that of your neighbor, coworker, uncle, brother, sister, or really anyone!

Think about your neighbors. No doubt their circumstances are different from yours. Now think about your family. How about your brother or sister? Even within a family, everyone has a unique situation. As an example, let me share mine. I have a mother and father, as well as three brothers and one sister. So far, you may say, that sounds normal, but let me explain further. My father was born on October 14, 1919. That's right, he was 52 years old when I was born. My younger brother was born when our father was 55 and my younger sister when he was 57! My mother is 19 years younger than my father. I have an older brother that is 8 years older than I am. My mother, in her first marriage, adopted him, and my father adopted him after marrying my mother. My oldest brother is 30 years older than I am. He is my half brother from my father's first marriage. All but one of his children—my nephews and niece—are older than I am. My parents were married in 1970 and, at the time of this writing, have just celebrated their 40th anniversary. My father is still pretty healthy and has just turned 91! On top of all this, my younger brother married my wife's younger sister. Pretty unique, right?

Naturally, you have your unique situation, too. Do you think the retirement needs for my family are different from yours? In all likelihood, they are. In addition to our family differences, we all have different thoughts and opinions for how things should be done. You may want to leave a sum of money to your children. Others may want to skip their children and leave an inheritance directly to their grandchildren. Some tell me that on the day they die they want to write their last check and that it should bounce. What is your goal? Most likely it has its own twist.

Regardless of what your goals may be, there are some commonalities and

Introduction

My purpose for writing this book is to assist individuals who are closing in on retirement, as well as those who are already retired. This book is for individuals looking for some guidance and trying to understand some of the complicated rules of retirement planning. It is for those who want some education to help them steer their family's financial ship. This is not meant to be a how-to guide or a master plan. It does not describe the most wonderful financial product known to man. It is not about loopholes to beat the government's tax plan. It is meant to be a resource for families facing different situations and with different goals. I want this book to be a source of knowledge that can empower the financial aspect of your retirement.

I have had the privilege of being in the financial services business for many years. Over those years, I have seen many rules and guidelines change. The financial world, in particular, changes rapidly. This is the main reason why this book can't be a how-to guide. The "how-to" constantly must be updated to stay current with changing rules. To have a successful retirement, I believe you need ongoing professional financial assistance from someone who specializes in retirement planning. You'll want advice from someone who keeps up with all the changes—which is a full-time job!

Family circumstances and financial solutions vary widely. No two families are the same and, therefore, I don't believe there can be a cookie cutter approach to financial planning or any one financial product that will work for everyone. I believe a personal approach is needed to create the outcome each individual family desires. This apin mind, that your neighbor's plan is not your plan. Just like you and your situation, your retirement plan should be unique. So let's get started now on learning some of the basics and helping you formulate your own unique financial plan!

Chapter 1

Understanding IRAs

Individual Retirement Arrangements (IRAs) have been utilized by millions of Americans who have socked away trillions of dollars in these types of savings vehicles. During the accumulation phase of life, people are thrilled to see their tax bills decrease and their balances grow as they contribute pre-tax dollars to these accounts. They have worked hard, saved for their future, and the balances in these accounts are the hard-earned result. When people enter the distribution phase—otherwise known as retirement—many questions arise about preserving wealth, making funds last, and perhaps even passing on an inheritance to their heirs.

IRAs can be confusing instruments, especially during the distribution phase. You may feel like you are navigating a maze and hitting walls or obstacles at every turn. This feeling is normal and occurs for good reason. The IRS publication that deals with the subject of IRAs (Publication 590) is 110 pages long. The rules for these accounts change regularly. What was true last year may not be true this year. In fact, the IRS publication starts off with an entire section entitled "What's New For..." the current year. Ed Slott, a leading IRA expert, says in his book, *The Retirement Savings Time Bomb... and How to Defuse It*, "Due to a complex combination of distribution and estate taxes that kick in at retirement or death, millions of you are at risk of losing much—perhaps even most—of your retirement savings."

If you are in or approaching the distribution phase, here are some of the questions you may have:

- Should I roll over my 401(k), 403(b), or other employer-provided retirement plan to an IRA?

- Should I wait until age 70 1/2 to take distributions?

- What if I want to leave my IRA to my children? What is the best way to do that?

- Doesn't my will or trust dictate where my IRA funds go after my death?

- How is settlement of an IRA inheritance handled?

- What are costly stretch IRA administrative mistakes every beneficiary needs to avoid?

It is important to be as focused during the distribution phase as you were during the accumulation phase. You worked hard to accumulate money into these accounts. Hopefully you reached the monetary goal you were aiming for. During distribution, your goal is to keep what you have earned. You might think about it this way: What good is it to make it to the summit if you lose everything on your way down?

Since IRA rules are always changing, you need to either be diligent in studying the rules or find a financial advisor who specializes in the various IRA accounts. Growing the money is important, but so is keeping it. An advisor who specializes in IRAs will be up-to-date on any changes and equipped to advise you. A good source for finding advisors with this specialty is the website, www.irahelp.com. Advisors listed on that site have immersed themselves in continuing education on IRAs.

The history of IRAs

Individual Retirement Arrangements were introduced with the Employee Retirement Income Security Act (ERISA) in 1974. IRAs allowed an income tax deduction for amounts placed into them and all interest earned in the account grew tax-deferred. Withdrawals of these funds were (and still are) considered taxable income to the owner during their life or the beneficiary upon inheritance.

Over time, variations of the IRA emerged. One of these is the non-deductible IRA. With this account, owners can make a contribution to the account and earn tax-deferred interest, but none of the contributions are tax deductible. The benefit is that the growth of the account is not taxable until withdrawn.

The Taxpayer Relief Act of 1997 brought about the next variation of the IRA—the Roth IRA. With a Roth account, participants make contributions to a personal retirement account and all earned interest is withdrawn tax-free at retirement. In addition, there is no mandatory withdrawal required of the Roth IRA other than at death. With a Roth IRA, there is no deduction allowed when contributions are made because these accounts are funded with after-tax dollars.

As the need for retirement savings increased, other plans were created like 401(a), 401(k), 457, SEP IRA, and others. These plans allow individuals to grow their retirement savings on a tax-deferred basis. All these plans result in taxable consequences for beneficiaries with the exception of the Roth IRA, which is income tax-free to both the owner and heirs upon withdrawal.

What is the Required Minimum Distribution?

The required minimum distribution (RMD) is the amount of money an owner of a traditional IRA is required to take out by April 1 following the year he or she reaches age 70 1/2 and by December 31 for every year after that. April 1 of the year after the year you reach age 70 1/2 is referred to as the required beginning date.

Distributions by the required beginning date

You must receive at least a minimum amount for each year starting with the year you reach age 70 1/2. If you do not (or did not) receive that minimum amount in your 70 1/2 year, then you must receive distributions for your 70 1/2 year by April 1 of the next year. If you do not take the distribution correctly you may have to pay a 50% excise tax on the amount not distributed as required. To calculate your RMD, the IRS provides distribution charts.

Which table to use to determine your Required Minimum Distribution
Table I (Single Life Expectancy). Use Table I (see p. 8) for years after the year of the owner's death if either of the following apply.

- You are an individual and a designated beneficiary, but not both the owner's surviving spouse and sole designated beneficiary.

- You are not an individual and the owner died on or after the required beginning date.

Surviving Spouse: If you are the owner's surviving spouse and sole designated beneficiary, and the owner had not reached age 70 1/2 when he or she died, and you do not elect to be treat-

IRS Publication 590 Table I
Single Life Expectancy (For Use By Beneficiaries)

Age	Life Expectancy	Age	Life Expectancy	Age	Life Expectancy	Age	Life Expectancy
0	82.4	28	55.3	56	28.7	84	8.1
1	81.6	29	54.3	57	27.9	85	7.6
2	80.6	30	53.3	58	27	86	7.1
3	79.7	31	52.4	59	26.1	87	6.7
4	78.7	32	51.4	60	25.2	88	6.3
5	77.7	33	50.4	61	24.4	89	5.9
6	76.7	34	49.4	62	23.5	90	5.5
7	75.8	35	48.5	63	22.7	91	5.2
8	74.8	36	47.5	64	21.8	92	4.9
9	73.8	37	46.5	65	21	93	4.6
10	72.8	38	45.6	66	20.2	94	4.3
11	71.8	39	44.6	67	19.4	95	4.1
12	70.8	40	43.6	68	18.6	96	3.8
13	69.9	41	42.7	69	17.8	97	3.6
14	68.9	42	41.7	70	17	98	3.4
15	67.9	43	40.7	71	16.3	99	3.1
16	66.9	44	39.8	72	15.5	100	2.9
17	66	45	38.8	73	14.8	101	2.7
18	65	46	37.9	74	14.1	102	2.5
19	64	47	37	75	13.4	103	2.3
20	63	48	36	76	12.7	104	2.1
21	62.1	49	35.1	77	12.1	105	1.9
22	61.1	50	34.2	78	11.4	106	1.7
23	60.1	51	33.3	79	10.8	107	1.5
24	59.1	52	32.3	80	10.2	108	1.4
25	58.2	53	31.4	81	9.7	109	1.2
26	57.2	54	30.5	82	9.1	110	1.1
27	56.2	55	29.6	83	8.6	111+	1

ed as the owner of the IRA, you do not have to take distributions (and use Table I on p. 8) until the year in which the owner would have reached age 70 1/2.

Table II (Joint Life and Last Survivor Expectancy). Use Table II (see Appendix A, p. 134-155) if you are the IRA owner and your spouse is both your sole designated beneficiary and more than 10 years younger than you.

Note: *Use this table in the year of the owner's death if the owner died after the required beginning date and this is the table that would have been used had he or she not died.*

Table III (Uniform Lifetime). Use Table III (see p. 10) if you are the IRA owner and your spouse is not both the sole designated beneficiary of your IRA and more than 10 years younger than you.

Note: *Use this table in the year of the owner's death if the owner died after the required beginning date and this is the table that would have been used had he or she not died.*

IRS Publication 590 Table III (Uniform Lifetime) (For Use by: Unmarried Owners, Married Owners Whose Spouses Are Not More Than 10 Years Younger, and Married Owners Whose Spouses Are Not the Sole Beneficiaries of Their IRAs)			
Age	Distribution Period	**Age**	Distribution Period
70	27.4	93	9.6
71	26.5	94	9.1
72	25.6	95	8.6
73	24.7	96	8.1
74	23.8	97	7.6
75	22.9	98	7.1
76	22.0	99	6.7
77	21.2	100	6.3
78	20.3	101	5.9
79	19.5	102	5.5
80	18.7	103	5.2
81	17.9	104	4.9
82	17.1	105	4.5
83	16.3	106	4.2
84	15.5	107	3.9
85	14.8	108	3.7
86	14.1	109	3.4
87	13.4	110	3.1
88	12.7	111	2.9
89	12.0	112	2.6
90	11.4	113	2.4
91	10.8	114	2.1
92	10.2	115+	1.9

Should I roll over my 401(k), 403(b), or other employer-provided retirement plan to an IRA?

If you have a 401(k), 403(b), or other company plan, but no longer work for the employer or intend on leaving soon, you may wonder about the best way to handle your company retirement account. You already may be aware of some available options. First, you can simply leave the account where it is. However, if the balance is not large your employer may require you to move the funds to another company plan or to an IRA. Which would be the best option for you? Some people believe that keeping their money in the company plan provides a group discount. Rarely is that the case, even if you work for a very large company. If you desire to be in control of your plan, have the most investment options, and control the amount of fees you pay, consider rolling over to an IRA. There are many reasons someone may consider rolling a 401(k) to an IRA. Listed below are a few reasons.

1. Your 401(k) investment options are limited. Most 401(k) plans offer few investment options. Sometimes you may only have nine or ten mutual fund options. A rollover to an IRA, on the other hand, opens up a world of investment options. These can number in the thousands. You can choose IRAs that will allow much more frequent trading than in the company plan. In an IRA, you can invest in mutual funds, individual stocks, exchange traded funds, annuities, CDs, money markets, and the list goes on.

2. A 401(k) plan cannot be stretched for non-spouse beneficiaries. If someone inherits a 401(k) and does not rollover to an inherited IRA, they will most likely have to pay all the taxes as a lump sum. However, with an inherited IRA rollover, the beneficiary can continue to defer taxes on a majority of the account. They are only required to take a minimum distribution. With a company plan, the company has a lot of power when it comes to the rules governing the plan. Even if the plan currently allows for setting up an account to "stretch" for the next generation, they can change the rules at any time.

3. With most 401(k) plans, you cannot convert to a Roth IRA. With the Roth IRA, money grows tax free. This can be a huge advantage if future tax rates go up. There eventually may be future tax laws that will allow for Roth IRA conversion from a 401(k), but with an IRA you own and control the account. Your previous employer cannot dictate how you handle your money once you convert your 401(k) to an IRA.

4. 401(k) plan fees are hard to understand. With a 401(k), the plan document is the rule book. The company chooses the investment options and what the fees will be. The government is working to make these fees more transparent, but do you want to allow your previous employer this much control over the fees you pay? With a rollover IRA, you manage not only the investment options but also the fees you pay. An IRA owner gets to write the rule book. The IRA owner is in control.

These are just a few of the reasons to rollover your employer-sponsored 401(k) into an IRA. I can think of only one reason not to rollover to an IRA. This applies to individuals between the ages of 55 and 59. At age 55, most 401(k) plans allow an individual to withdraw funds without a 10% tax penalty. With IRAs, you have to be 59 1/2 to withdraw without a tax penalty. So, if you are in that age group and you will need income from the account, it may wise to leave your funds in the company plan.

How to do a 401(k) rollover

The next logical question is, "How do I complete a rollover?" It's a great question. 401(k) rollovers can seem intimidating. There a few things to be considered. First, where do you want the IRA to be held? The IRA will need a custodian, which basically means what company or financial institution will hold the IRA. There are many options. Some popular ones are Schwab, Fidelity, Scot-trade, or TD Ameritrade. It could be your local bank or credit union. Most of the time, you will open an account with a new custodian first. Once you have done this, you will contact your current 401(k) provider. Sometimes you will be able to start the transfer right over the phone. There some providers that will require you to fill out a rollover form. I always recommend that my clients do a trustee-to-trustee transfer. You will have to indicate to where the employer-sponsored account is being transferred, which will be to your new or existing IRA account. The good news is that, if done correctly, the IRS allows individuals to rollover their company plan to an IRA without triggering a tax!

Do a trustee-to-trustee transfer

- A trustee-to-trustee transfer means the check for the funds in your employer-sponsored account is made out to the new institution with which you are setting up your IRA.

- When you do a trustee-to-trustee transfer there is no limit to the amount of transfers you can do.

- If you do what is called a "60-day rollover," you are limited to only one rollover per year.

60-day rollover rule

- This applies when the check for the funds in the employer-sponsored account is made out to you.

- There will be a mandatory 20% tax withholding.

- You must deposit the funds in an IRA within 60 days from the receipt of the funds. There are no exceptions.

- Funds not deposited within 60 days are considered income and subject to tax and penalty.

While this may seems foreign to you, just remember it is really not that hard and most financial institutions or financial planners can guide you through this process. When completed you will have your own plan and not a company plan; you will be in control of your financial future.

Should I wait until age 70 1/2 to take distributions?

Questions arise around the subject of required minimum distributions. One question often raised is when should I start to take my distributions? Obviously, the answer varies based on personal circumstances. There are things you should consider.

Assume you are age 60 and have $500,000 in your IRA. If you earn a modest 6% rate of return, your account value will be $895,423 at age 70. Using Table III (see p. 10) to calculate your RMD, you would take $895,423 and divide it by your life expectancy at age 70, which is 27.4 years according to the table. This means your required distribution will be $32,679.67 ($895,423 ÷ 27.4). This amount will add to your adjusted gross income and could put you into a higher tax bracket.

Extending your distributions over a longer timeframe would help you avoid such a big jump in income. For example, assume you started taking $20,000 per year from the IRA at age 60 and converted those funds to a Roth IRA. The Roth IRA allows your money to grow tax free and there are no RMDs. At age 70, your traditional IRA will have approximately $635,000 and your RMD will be $23,175. This could potentially keep you in a lower tax bracket. In addition, you would also have a Roth IRA with a balance of $275,000, equaling a grand total between the two accounts of $910,000! This would require you to pay some tax along the way, but it is important to understand that someone will eventually pay those taxes. This strategy is not advisable if you feel future taxes will be lower. However, it is a strategy to consider if, like me and most other Americans, you believe future taxes will almost certainly be higher.

What if I want to leave my IRA to my children? What is the best way to do that?

When an IRA passes to the next generation, it is the beneficiary, not the original owner or the estate, who is responsible for the taxes due on the inheritance. IRAs and retirement accounts have a different set of tax rules than real estate, savings accounts, or even stocks.

IRA inheritance income taxes are generally a shocking surprise, as most families have never discussed the matter. In fact, many IRA owners are not even aware they are leaving something behind that can cause so much trouble. For beneficiaries, the IRA they receive could be reduced by 40% or more due to taxes. This could be prevented with some education about inherited IRAs.

When the IRA inheritance is withdrawn immediately, the taxes can create immediate and catastrophic losses of wealth. The additional income the inheritance creates can also compound the beneficiary's personal taxes by pushing them into a higher tax bracket when added to their other household income. It is not uncommon to see up to 40% or more of an inherited IRA immediately handed over to the government in taxes. I don't have to tell you this, but losing nearly half of your inheritance and later finding out you could have avoided that loss is not pleasant!

What is a stretch IRA?

Beneficiaries can use today's tax laws to their advantage. Current tax laws allow a beneficiary to avoid liquidating an IRA. This means the IRA can continue to grow tax-deferred over their lives. The only stipulation is that they must take a required minimum distribution annually. The financial implications of this method—the stretch IRA—are considerable. The stretch IRA is also commonly called the generational IRA or inherited IRA. All of these terms mean the same thing.

By continuing tax deferral, the inherited IRA continues to compound. This allows a beneficiary to turn an inheritance into a substantial stream of income relative to their life expectancy. Most of the time, IRS tax tables—such as Table I (Single Life Expectancy, see p. 8)—are used to calculate life expectancies for IRA beneficiaries. For younger beneficiaries, the long-term benefits can be huge. The reason is that they have a much longer life expectancy.

You can turn your IRA into a multi-generational lifetime of benefit by using the stretch IRA

"Compound interest is the eighth wonder of the world." That quote has been attributed—falsely—to such notable thinkers as Benjamin Franklin, Albert Einstein, and John Maynard Keynes. No matter who said it first, there is no doubt that compounding is powerful. Trillions of dollars sit in IRAs today because that money has been able to compound tax-deferred. Beneficiaries who inherit IRAs as stretch IRAs may be able to perpetuate the benefits of tax deferment over the course of their lives. It is even possible to chan-

nel these funds into a substantial legacy of income for themselves and their
families.

Consider an example. Judy is 45
years old. She just inherited her mother's $350,000 IRA. Before inheriting
the IRA, she was in the 25% marginal
tax bracket. Judy currently works. She
has two children. One is currently entering college and the other will enter
college in two years. Judy will need additional income to pay for college. She
is also planning for her own retirement
income needs.

If Judy does what most beneficiaries do and takes a full distribution of
her mother's IRA account, it will trigger a few negative events. She will no
longer be in the 25% tax bracket; the
distribution will push her into the 35%
tax bracket. She will immediately lose
$122,500 of the $350,000 to taxes. That
money and the earnings it could have
generated in her lifetime will be lost
forever. Consider the effect of losing
out on the compounded growth of those
funds. If Judy could had saved the

$122,500 and earned only 5%, it would have grown to $325,028 by the time she turned 65. Consider this also: because Judy did not have the knowledge she needed, she lost her inheritance of a tax-deferred IRA account. Had she known how to utilize the inherited IRA she could have withdrawn money any time without incurring a federal excise tax penalty. This is something she cannot do with her own IRA accounts.

Now let's consider the brighter scenario. If Judy inherits her mother's IRA and utilizes a stretch IRA, she will be in control over the entire balance in the account. Judy will have the power to choose when and how much she will take each year as long as she fulfills the required minimum distribution. She will be required to take an annual distribution from the account once each year and her first year distribution will be $9,020.62. This is based on the $350,000 value and her age. The $9,020.62 will be added to her income. Most likely, the additional income will not push her into a higher tax bracket.

If Judy earns only a 6% rate of return and lives until age 85, the sum total distributions over her lifetime will equal $1,232,304.58!

But what if Judy dies before age 85? Her beneficiaries can continue stretching their inherited IRA account in the same manner. Distributions from the account would continue using Judy's life expectancy. For this to happen, Judy would have to make sure she has named beneficiaries to her inherited IRA. This would put Judy's inherited IRA into overdrive!

The tax-free benefits of an inherited Roth IRA

When viewed as a financial investment, the Roth IRA can be extremely valuable. Few people grasp the implications or potential of these accounts to their heirs when they are inherited as a stretch Roth IRA. It adds up to a great deal more than simply leaving an inheritance tax-free. When passed to the next generation, a stretch Roth IRA can continue to compound

Inherited IRA Example—45-year-old

Age	Beginning Account Value	IRS Divisor	RMD $	Ending Value
	Amount Inherited $350,000		Interest Earned 6%	
45	$350,000.00	38.8	$9,020.62	$340,979.38
46	$361,979.38	37.9	$9,550.91	$352,428.47
47	$374,147.24	37.0	$10,112.09	$364,035.15
48	$386,483.98	36.1	$10,705.93	$375,778.06
49	$398,967.10	35.1	$11,366.58	$387,600.51
50	$411,538.54	34.2	$12,033.29	$399,505.25
51	$424,197.56	33.3	$12,738.67	$411,458.89
52	$436,910.75	32.3	$13,526.65	$423,384.10
53	$449,598.74	31.4	$14,318.43	$435,280.31
54	$462,256.24	30.5	$15,155.94	$447,100.29
55	$474,835.67	29.6	$16,041.75	$458,793.92
56	$487,284.06	28.7	$16,978.54	$470,305.52
57	$499,542.57	27.9	$17,904.75	$481,637.82
58	$511,610.37	27.0	$18,948.53	$492,661.84
59	$523,358.46	26.1	$20,052.05	$503,306.41
60	$534,707.92	25.2	$21,218.57	$513,489.35
61	$545,571.83	24.4	$22,359.50	$523,212.33
62	$555,946.64	23.5	$23,657.30	$532,289.33
63	$565,646.13	22.7	$24,918.33	$540,727.80
64	$574,666.57	21.8	$26,360.85	$548,305.71
65	$582,785.71	21.0	$27,751.70	$555,034.01
66	$590,001.15	20.2	$29,207.98	$560,793.17
67	$596,193.24	19.4	$30,731.61	$565,461.63
68	$601,233.23	18.6	$32,324.37	$568,908.86
69	$604,982.85	17.8	$33,987.80	$570,995.05
70	$607,294.02	17.0	$35,723.18	$571,570.85
71	$608,008.49	16.3	$37,301.13	$570,707.35
72	$607,187.86	15.5	$39,173.41	$568,014.45
73	$604,445.72	14.8	$40,840.93	$563,604.80
74	$599,871.54	14.1	$42,544.08	$557,327.46
75	$593,319.75	13.4	$44,277.59	$549,042.16
76	$584,641.34	12.7	$46,034.75	$538,606.59
77	$573,685.07	12.1	$47,411.99	$526,273.08
78	$560,694.19	11.4	$49,183.70	$511,510.49
79	$545,152.14	10.8	$50,477.05	$494,675.09
80	$527,384.22	10.2	$51,704.33	$475,679.88
81	$507,322.93	9.7	$52,301.33	$455,021.60
82	$485,460.98	9.1	$53,347.36	$432,113.62
83	$461,241.27	8.6	$53,632.71	$407,608.57
84	$435,283.04	8.1	$53,738.65	$381,544.40
85	$407,661.38	7.6	$53,639.66	$354,021.72
Total Distribution			$1,232,304.58	

and grow tax -free just as it did during the life of the original owner.

Like a regular inherited IRA, a required minimum distribution must be taken from the account using the IRS Table I for IRA beneficiaries (see p. 8). The major difference is that distributions from an inherited Roth IRA are income tax-free to the beneficiaries! Even if taken as a full distribution, the withdrawals are tax-free. The major problem is that most beneficiaries do not keep the funds in a Roth. They simply make a lump sum withdrawal. When this is done, they lose the power of tax-free growth!

Consider that all earnings inside an inherited Roth IRA account and all distributed income from the account are tax-free to the beneficiary. Suppose you are the beneficiary and you are quite good at investing. You inherit $10,000 from a Roth IRA and through wise investments, you turn it into $500,000. The entire $500,000 is tax-free upon withdrawal! This clearly demonstrates the true value of an inherited stretch Roth IRA.

Six powerful reasons for executing a stretch IRA

1. Allows beneficiaries to flexibly time their withdrawals. Under the stretch method, the beneficiary must take an annual required minimum distribution. The remaining funds can stay in the account growing tax-deferred. Say you are a beneficiary, but in a given tax year you experienced losses from other activities. If you actively manage your taxes, it is possible to take a larger withdrawal from the IRA in order to offset those losses. The beneficiary can benefit from a tax-free withdrawal from inherited tax-deferred wealth.

2. Provides an account that beneficiaries cannot buy. If a beneficiary is under age 59 1/2, inheriting an IRA account would be an extremely valuable financial instrument, as it is something he or she cannot buy. Individuals younger than 59 1/2 cannot withdraw funds from regular tax-deferred retirement accounts without incurring a penalty; however, if they inherit one, there would be no federal excise taxes on the withdrawals. An inherited IRA provides a tax-deferred account to beneficiaries in which they can manage their inherited IRA wealth without any tax consequences. If the inheritance is from a Roth IRA, then it is tax-free.

3. Allows beneficiaries to control taxes. If a beneficiary takes a full distribution of an inherited IRA, they lose multiple wealth preservation and creation opportunities. In addition, at the time of full distribution, they provide a tax windfall to the IRS. The entire sum may be fully subject to taxes, and sole control to time the taxation is lost.

For a beneficiary who is working and earning a sufficient income, there may be no need for the income provided by the inherited required minimum distributions. Once retired, however, the beneficiary may need to increase the withdrawals for a higher level of income. By properly managing the inherited stretch IRA, the beneficiary preserves control of withdrawals above the required minimum distribution amount.

4. Offers beneficiaries a way to minimize current taxes. It often comes as a nasty surprise to beneficiaries of inherited IRA accounts that a taxable distribution may increase their total taxes due. Taking a full distribution may require paying higher taxes on all household income. The taxable distribution is added to all other income, which means personal income taxes may increase. This can come as a blow to uninformed beneficiaries.

5. Supplies beneficiaries with an inheritance of a personal retirement account. The inheritance of an IRA account is an invaluable financial instrument of retirement planning for the beneficiary. The inherited stretch IRA has even more benefits than a personal IRA. The inheritance of an IRA account and use of the stretch method offers more than an inheritance. For beneficiaries, it can provide financial peace of mind and an added measure of security for their own retirement as well.

6. Perpetuates a family legacy. Many times, beneficiaries feel no physical, emotional, or spiritual connection to an inheritance. Without these connections, rarely does an inheritance last past the second generation. With the stretch method, beneficiaries can preserve and perpetuate their inherited tax-deferred wealth until the end of their lives. Their families and descendents can enjoy the legacy created through the discipline and sacrifice of their parents and benefactors.

Doesn't my will or trust dictate where my IRA funds go after my death?

The short answer is no. The distribution of IRA funds is governed by the beneficiary form regardless of whom your will or trust names as your heirs.

Properly naming primary and contingent beneficiaries

Your IRA assets can be considerably diminished by probate costs and excessive taxes if you do not have a properly named beneficiary. You must name two categories of beneficiaries: primary and contingent.

Upon the owner's death, the account is divided among the primary beneficiaries. The division may be by a dollar amount indicated on the beneficiary election form or by percentage. If the type of division has not been indicated, the financial institution typically divides the account evenly among all living primary beneficiaries.

If there are no living primary beneficiaries, the funds are paid to contingent beneficiaries. If no contingent beneficiary has been named, the account goes to the estate and enters probate. Be certain you have named a contingent beneficiary on your tax-deferred retirement accounts. In the case of couples with children, the spouse will be named the primary beneficiary and the children as contingent beneficiaries.

Per stirpes

Can you accidentally disinherit a loved one? Absolutely! By not using per capita or per stirpes designations, it is possible that your IRA may not go to the family or persons you intended.

How could this happen? Let's consider an example. Say you have two children, Tim and Catherine. Tim has four children and Catherine has none. While Tim and Catherine are alive, your IRA would be split evenly between them when you die. However, your intention is for Tim's share of the inherited IRA to go to his children if Tim dies before you do. If Tim dies first and then you die, without any special notation on the IRA beneficiary form, your grandchildren would be disinherited and the entire IRA would go to Catherine.

To prevent this from happening, use the words per stirpes after Tim's name on the beneficiary designation form. Without this notation, the IRA will pass per capita and will be shared among the other living beneficiaries.

Per capita

As the example above demonstrated, it is easy to unwittingly disinherit a beneficiary. Most financial institutions assume a per capita distribution, meaning they will pay the IRA only to living beneficiaries upon the owner's death. If Tim and Catherine had no children, the issue of per capita or per stirpes would be of no concern.

The key takeaway of this is that most financial institutions assume per capita designations unless otherwise indicated. Speak with a legal professional if you need more information. Be sure to review beneficiary designations whenever a death in the family occurs.

Living trusts and IRAs

Most families assume a living trust will manage the entire estate burden a family faces upon the death of a loved one. For IRA accounts, this is not true.

A living trust has many purposes. A correctly drafted living trust can protect your estate from federal estate taxes. These are the taxes assessed by the government on the entire estate. Beyond estate taxes, income taxes on IRA accounts are due and payable by the beneficiary no matter what the size of the estate. You may need to consult an estate advisor to determine if estate taxes will be a concern for you.

The primary function of trusts is to protect from probate any assets that do not automatically bypass. A trust may help avoid probate on assets like homes, brokerage accounts, investment properties, and bank accounts. If you have properly named a beneficiary for your IRA, it likely will avoid the probate process.

Some exceptions

You may have a good reason to name a trust as the beneficiary, but you must have your trust specially drafted to take full advantage of this. One reason might be a special needs child who will require a trustee to administer funds. Another reason you may want your trustee to control the distributions is that you do not wish to hand over full control to your heirs. Yet another reason may be that you have a very large estate.

Leaving an IRA to charity

If you are charitably inclined, it can be beneficial to leave your tax-deferred wealth to charity at death instead of other appreciated assets. Assets like real estate receive a step up in tax basis at death. Because of this, there are no taxes due upon the sale or liquidation of assets at your death. On the other hand, tax-deferred IRAs have taxes due on the account at death. The beneficiary is responsible for those taxes.

If you plan to donate a portion of your estate to charity, consider leaving an IRA. Charities typically do not pay taxes. This means they would not owe taxes upon inheritance of these accounts. You can avoid giving an asset with a tax liability to your family by bequeathing your tax-deferred IRA to charity.

If a family change has occurred, update your beneficiary forms

Death, birth, divorce, remarriage. These are common changes that occur in a family. If one of these changes takes place, review your beneficiary elections on your retirement accounts. Many times children or grandchildren are born after beneficiary forms are filled out. If this happens, update your beneficiary designations so that no one is accidentally excluded.

Discuss IRA inheritance with your heirs now

If beneficiaries are unprepared, inheriting an IRA can be financially taxing and disappointing. Beneficiaries are responsible for the taxes due on these accounts. This may come as a big and unwelcome surprise.

Additionally, an inherited tax-deferred retirement account can push your heirs into a higher tax bracket.

In fact, depending on the size of the account, your beneficiaries could be pushed into the highest federal income tax bracket. If your state has an income tax, that would be an added expense. Discuss this with your heirs now so they will be prepared when the time comes.

How is an IRA inheritance settled?

To begin settling IRA accounts, the estate executor, trustee, or beneficiary should contact the financial institution that holds the accounts. Financial institutions have different procedures for settling IRA accounts.

Most require a certified death certificate. Once the financial institution has verified that a death has occurred, they will start contacting and corresponding with the account's named beneficiaries.

Note: *If there are multiple beneficiaries, it is essential that accounts are segregated into separate accounts before any distributions are made. Failure to do so can result in a loss of the* *stretch IRA and subsequent income tax benefits.*

After accounts are segregated, beneficiaries can decide how to settle their individual shares.

Probate

IRA accounts can avoid probate if beneficiaries have been properly designated. The IRA funds will pass directly to named beneficiaries.

Year of death required minimum distribution. After reaching age 70 1/2, IRA owners must take an annual required minimum distribution from their account. If the owner of the IRA died before taking the annual required minimum distribution, a distribution has to be taken from the account and paid to the beneficiary, who is then responsible for the taxes on the distribution. You must contact the financial institution to determine if the annual distribution has taken place.

If the IRA was a Roth IRA, no minimum distributions is required for the deceased owner; however, a non-spouse beneficiary must withdraw the minimum required amount to satisfy the stretch Roth IRA rules and avoid tax penalties.

Beneficiary determination date. By September 30 of the year following the year of death, all beneficiaries must be finalized. This is necessary so that each can determine the required minimum distribution under the stretch IRA. This is referred to as the designation date. The purpose of this deadline is to give beneficiaries the opportunity to decide if they want to disclaim or decline their share of the IRA inheritance.

Proper segregation of the IRA. The IRA account must be segregated into separate accounts representing each beneficiary's share by December 31 of the year after the death of the IRA owner. This is necessary so that each beneficiary can take advantage of the stretch IRA provision using his or her own age. If the account has not been segregated by this date, the minimum required distribution for the entire account will be determined by the age of the oldest beneficiary. This can be a disadvantage when beneficiaries have a wide disparity in age as the younger beneficiaries will have to draw out much more than they would have otherwise been required had the account been properly segregated. Additionally, this will create an unnecessary tax burden for younger beneficiaries.

Qualified disclaimers. If a beneficiary wants to disclaim an IRA inheritance, it must be done in writing and generally by September 30 of the year of the IRA owner's death.

The option of disclaiming an inheritance may be chosen to allow families to better manage wealth within the family. This strategy allows a beneficiary to pass some or all of an inherited IRA to the next named beneficiary.

As an example, a father could name his daughter as a primary beneficiary and her children (his grandchildren) as contingent beneficiaries. If the daughter was well-off financially and had no need for the inheritance of the IRA, she could disclaim it. As contingent beneficiaries, it would pass on to her children.

Assuming the daughter had a large estate or no need for the funds from the inheritance, the disclaimer would allow her to avoid increasing her estate and potentially increasing her tax burden. Naturally, the daughter's children would have a longer life expectancy, so the stretch IRA calculated over their lives could considerably increase the amount of lifetime income distributions.

The decision to disclaim should not be made lightly. A disclaimer is an irrevocable decision to give up your right to inherit IRA assets. You cannot change your mind once that decision has been executed.

Note: *The primary beneficiary does not get to choose the person they wish to disclaim to. Whoever ultimately receives the IRA inheritance is dictated by the beneficiaries named on the beneficiary election form when the owner died. If the primary beneficiary disclaims the* *inheritance, it will go to the next listed contingent beneficiary.*

Settlement options when the spouse is the primary beneficiary of an IRA

There are four inheritance options when a spouse is the beneficiary of the IRA and the owner dies.

1. Spousal continuation. This option allows the account to be continued and retitled to the name of the surviving spouse. If the spouse who died was taking required minimum distributions at the time of his or her death and was over the age of 70 1/2, then the required distribution must be made before rolling the account into the name of the surviving spouse. After the rollover, the surviving spouse will use his or her age to determine the required minimum distributions. No distribution is required for a Roth IRA under this method.

2. Stretch IRA. The spouse may receive the account as an inherited (stretch) IRA and take distributions using the single life expectancy table.

This is the table provided by the IRS and used by beneficiaries to stretch the IRA distributions over their life expectancy. Surviving spouses who elect this option do not have to take a distribution until the year after the year of the IRA owner's death or the year the IRA owner would have turned 70 1/2, whichever is later.

3. Use disclaimers. A spouse named as primary beneficiary has the right to disclaim some or all of the IRA assets and pass them on to the next generation. Before choosing this option, be sure to review who is listed as beneficiaries and complete a new beneficiary election form.

4. Full liquidation. A spouse can close (liquidate) the account. There will be no taxes if the account is a Roth IRA. Unless funds are needed, this may not be the wisest option. Closing the account may lead to the loss of benefits that could be derived from other options.

IRA settlement options for non-spouse beneficiaries

Children, siblings, parents, and friends may be listed as non-spouse beneficiaries to an IRA account. There are four basic distribution options open to non-spouse beneficiaries of an IRA.

1. Full liquidation. Beneficiaries can choose to cash out their IRA inheritance. This distribution is considered income, which will be added to the rest of the beneficiary's household income unless it is a Roth IRA. Taxes will be due and payable. Electing the lump sum cash out can push the beneficiary into a higher tax bracket and result in a surprising and unwelcome tax bill.

This option eliminates any benefits that could be derived from tax deferring the inheritance over the life of the beneficiary and all the benefits of an inherited stretch IRA.

2. Five-year deferral. Beneficiaries can lose the opportunity to inherit the account as a stretch IRA if they elect not to settle their IRA inheritance by December 31 of the year following the death of the owner. If they make this choice, they are subject to the five-year rule, which requires full liquidation of the account within five years. The five-year rule does not apply if the owner of the IRA was 70 1/2 or older at the time of death.

3. Stretch IRA. The third option is, after inheritance, to leave the IRA in its tax-deferred state. You will be required to take an annual minimum distributions over your life expectancy. You can always take more than the minimum, but you must take at least the minimum distribution each year. This option allows the beneficiary to avoid a large income tax bill and means the inheritance may grow into a significantly larger sum of money. The annual distribution is calculated based on your life expectancy using IRS tables for IRA beneficiaries.

As has already been discussed, the benefit of the stretch IRA is that it provides you with the most withdrawal flexibility. Even more importantly, you could end up with significantly more money over your lifetime due to the continued tax-deferred status of the account. Especially for tax-free Roth IRAs, this can be a significant benefit.

4. Use disclaimers. This option allows the primary beneficiary to pass on some or all of the IRA to the named contingent beneficiaries, who can then inherit the account as a stretch IRA.

How to calculate the stretch IRA

If you elect to distribute your inherited IRA by using the stretch option, you will be required to take a minimum annual withdrawal from the account for the rest of your life. This withdrawal is determined by the value of the account and the life expectancy of the beneficiary as established by the IRS in Table I (see p. 8). The beneficiary must take the required minimum distribution to avoid penalties. The beneficiary may always take more than the minimum if needed, but they must take at least the minimum withdrawal to avoid penalties. The financial institution where the IRA is held may allow distributions to occur annually, monthly, or quarterly.

To calculate the full annual required minimum distribution, the beneficiary will use the value of the inherited IRA as of December 31 of the previous year and then divide it by the life expectancy factor listed in Table I (see p. 8).

Here is an example

Value of owner's IRA as of
Dec. 31 .... $192,542.25
Age of beneficiary 52
Assumed rate of return 6%
Life expectancy factor from
Table I for a 52-year-old 32.3
Required minimum distribution
(RMD) calculation .. $192,542.25 ÷ 32.3
Required minimum
distribution $5,961.06

Beneficiaries will use their own life expectancy and the inherited account value when making the RMD calculation. To determine what the next year's RMD would be, the beneficiary would use the divider from Table I (see p. 8)

Inherited IRA Example—52-year-old

Age	Amount Inherited $192,542.25 Beginning Account Value	IRS Divisor	Interest Earned 6% RMD $	Ending Value
52	$192,542.25	32.3	$5,961.06	$186,581.19
53	$198,133.72	31.4	$6,309.99	$191,823.73
54	$203,711.76	30.5	$6,679.07	$197,032.68
55	$209,255.39	29.6	$7,069.44	$202,185.95
56	$214,741.27	28.7	$7,482.27	$207,259.00
57	$220,143.47	27.9	$7,890.45	$212,253.03
58	$225,461.64	27.0	$8,350.43	$217,111.21
59	$230,638.90	26.1	$8,836.74	$221,802.16
60	$235,640.50	25.2	$9,350.81	$226,289.68
61	$240,428.11	24.4	$9,853.61	$230,574.50
62	$245,000.19	23.5	$10,425.54	$234,574.65
63	$249,274.66	22.7	$10,981.26	$238,293.40
64	$253,249.88	21.8	$11,616.97	$241,632.91
65	$256,827.90	21.0	$12,229.90	$244,598.00
66	$260,007.68	20.2	$12,871.67	$247,136.01
67	$262,736.47	19.4	$13,543.12	$249,193.35
68	$264,957.54	18.6	$14,245.03	$250,712.51
69	$266,609.97	17.8	$14,978.09	$251,631.88
70	$267,628.48	17.0	$15,742.85	$251,885.62
71	$267,943.33	16.3	$16,438.24	$251,505.09
72	$267,581.69	15.5	$17,263.33	$250,318.36
73	$266,373.26	14.8	$17,998.19	$248,375.07
74	$264,357.46	14.1	$18,748.76	$245,608.71
75	$261,470.15	13.4	$19,512.70	$241,957.45
76	$257,645.66	12.7	$20,287.06	$237,358.60
77	$252,817.34	12.1	$20,894.00	$231,923.35
78	$247,092.39	11.4	$21,674.77	$225,417.62
79	$240,243.16	10.8	$22,244.74	$217,998.42
80	$232,413.01	10.2	$22,785.59	$209,627.42
81	$223,572.20	9.7	$23,048.68	$200,523.52
82	$213,937.86	9.1	$23,509.65	$190,428.20
83	$203,264.47	8.6	$23,635.40	$179,629.07
84	$191,824.94	8.1	$23,682.09	$168,142.85
85	$179,652.34	7.6	$23,638.47	$156,013.88
Total Distribution			$509,779.98	

each year that corresponds with their current age.

In this same example, if the beneficiary was a 12-year-old grandson, the factor from Table I (see p. 8) would be 70.8 and the RMD would only be $2,761.90.

Let's look at the full benefits of the stretch IRA. If these accounts earned 6% for the entire life of the beneficiary who we will estimate to live to age 85, the 52-year-old would receive a total of $509,780 from the required minimum distributions and would still have a balance in the inherited IRA of $156,013.38

In the example of the 12-year-old grandson, he would receive a total of $2,850,436 in distributions and at age 85 there would still be a balance of $742,060.77! This represents what 73 years of tax-deferred compounding power can do.

Inherited IRA Example—12-year-old

Age	Amount Inherited $192,542.25		Interest Earned 6%	
	Beginning Account Value	IRS Divisor	RMD $	Ending Value
12	$192,542.25	70.8	$2,719.52	$189,822.73
13	$201,375.26	69.9	$2,880.91	$198,494.36
14	$210,576.87	68.9	$3,056.27	$207,520.60
15	$220,155.22	67.9	$3,242.34	$216,912.87
16	$230,122.18	66.9	$3,439.79	$226,682.39
17	$240,489.72	66.0	$3,643.78	$236,845.94
18	$251,275.32	65.0	$3,865.77	$247,409.55
19	$262,486.07	64.0	$4,101.34	$258,384.72
20	$274,133.89	63.0	$4,351.33	$269,782.55
21	$286,230.59	62.1	$4,609.19	$281,621.40
22	$298,795.24	61.1	$4,890.27	$293,904.97
23	$311,832.68	60.1	$5,188.56	$306,644.12
24	$325,354.08	59.1	$5,505.15	$319,848.94
25	$339,370.18	58.2	$5,831.10	$333,539.08
26	$353,901.29	57.2	$6,187.09	$347,714.20
27	$368,948.28	56.2	$6,564.92	$362,383.36
28	$384,520.26	55.3	$6,953.35	$377,566.91
29	$400,638.13	54.3	$7,378.23	$393,259.89
30	$417,298.18	53.3	$7,829.23	$409,468.95
31	$434,506.84	52.4	$8,292.12	$426,214.72
32	$452,285.13	51.4	$8,799.32	$443,485.81
33	$470,622.92	50.4	$9,337.76	$461,285.16
34	$489,522.54	49.4	$9,909.36	$479,613.17
35	$508,984.53	48.5	$10,494.53	$498,490.00
36	$529,029.07	47.5	$11,137.45	$517,891.62
37	$549,633.36	46.5	$11,820.07	$537,813.29
38	$570,791.29	45.6	$12,517.35	$558,273.94
39	$592,521.41	44.6	$13,285.23	$579,236.18
40	$614,787.47	43.6	$14,100.63	$600,686.84
41	$637,574.08	42.7	$14,931.48	$622,642.61
42	$660,897.05	41.7	$15,848.85	$645,048.20
43	$684,702.02	40.7	$16,823.15	$667,878.88
44	$708,961.00	39.8	$17,813.09	$691,147.91
45	$733,685.57	38.8	$18,909.42	$714,776.15
46	$758,797.28	37.9	$20,021.04	$738,776.25
47	$784,304.08	37.0	$21,197.41	$763,106.68
48	$810,164.92	36.0	$22,504.58	$787,660.34
49	$836,270.23	35.1	$23,825.36	$812,444.87

Inherited IRA Example—12-year-old (continued)

Age	Beginning Account Value	IRS Divisor	RMD $	Ending Value
	Amount Inherited $192,542.25		**Interest Earned** 6%	
50	$862,621.09	34.2	$25,222.84	$837,398.25
51	$889,155.51	33.3	$26,701.37	$862,454.15
52	$915,803.48	32.3	$28,353.05	$887,450.43
53	$942,398.64	31.4	$30,012.70	$912,385.94
54	$968,929.86	30.5	$31,768.19	$937,161.67
55	$995,297.46	29.6	$33,624.91	$961,672.54
56	$1,021,390.39	28.7	$35,588.52	$985,801.88
57	$1,047,085.30	27.9	$37,529.94	$1,009,555.36
58	$1,072,380.48	27.0	$39,717.80	$1,032,662.68
59	$1,097,005.51	26.1	$42,030.86	$1,054,974.65
60	$1,120,794.98	25.2	$44,475.99	$1,076,318.99
61	$1,143,566.69	24.4	$46,867.49	$1,096,699.20
62	$1,165,313.20	23.5	$49,587.80	$1,115,725.41
63	$1,185,644.20	22.7	$52,231.02	$1,133,413.18
64	$1,204,551.83	21.8	$55,254.67	$1,149,297.16
65	$1,221,570.27	21.0	$58,170.01	$1,163,400.25
66	$1,236,694.47	20.2	$61,222.50	$1,175,471.97
67	$1,249,673.64	19.4	$64,416.17	$1,185,257.47
68	$1,260,237.89	18.6	$67,754.73	$1,192,483.17
69	$1,268,097.44	17.8	$71,241.43	$1,196,856.01
70	$1,272,941.86	17.0	$74,878.93	$1,198,062.92
71	$1,274,439.43	16.3	$78,186.47	$1,196,252.97
72	$1,272,719.33	15.5	$82,110.92	$1,190,608.41
73	$1,266,971.57	14.8	$85,606.19	$1,181,365.38
74	$1,257,383.67	14.1	$89,176.15	$1,168,207.53
75	$1,243,650.55	13.4	$92,809.74	$1,150,840.81
76	$1,225,459.84	12.7	$96,492.90	$1,128,966.94
77	$1,202,494.53	12.1	$99,379.71	$1,103,114.82
78	$1,175,264.49	11.4	$103,093.38	$1,072,171.11
79	$1,142,686.98	10.8	$105,804.35	$1,036,882.63
80	$1,105,443.85	10.2	$108,376.85	$997,067.00
81	$1,063,393.63	9.7	$109,628.21	$953,765.42
82	$1,017,569.04	9.1	$111,820.77	$905,748.27
83	$966,802.41	8.6	$112,418.88	$854,383.52
84	$912,391.67	8.1	$112,640.95	$799,750.72
85	$854,494.22	7.6	$112,433.45	$742,060.77
Total Distribution			**$2,850,436.18**	

If choosing the stretch IRA option, what costly administrative mistakes should every beneficiary avoid?

There are many potential pitfalls for non-spouse beneficiaries who inherit IRAs. Even when they have the best intentions, they may find themselves snared by these traps.

Rolling an inherited IRA into an existing IRA in the belief they have avoided taxes on their inheritance. This is the most common mistake beneficiaries make. When inheriting the IRA as a stretch IRA, it cannot be rolled over to a personal IRA. The account must be segregated and list the proper registration as a descendent IRA.

Inherited and personal IRAs cannot be co-mingled. The proper registration of a stretch IRA looks like the following: **John Jones IRA deceased, FBO of Jimmy Jones, beneficiary.** (FBO means "for the benefit of.")

Without the name of the decedent on it, the account is not a qualified inherited stretch IRA and it could be challenged by the IRS.

Avoiding double taxation. If the estate from which you inherited the IRA paid federal estate taxes, you may be eligible for a tax deduction on your inherited IRA. This tax phenomenon is called "income in respect of the decedent." See an estate attorney or tax advisor for guidance on this issue.

Caution about brokerage accounts. When a brokerage firm is notified of an IRA investor's death, the account is frozen. This means that no transactions can occur until the new owners/beneficiaries are identified and the account has been divided accordingly. If the account is invested in volatile financial instruments, the beneficiaries possibly could experience a loss in the account between the time the institution is notified of the death and their eventual inheritance. Because of this, time is of the essence when settling these accounts.

Changing inherited IRA custodians. After inheriting an IRA, you may realize the account investments do not match your family's financial goals and objectives. Additionally, you may have inherited multiple IRAs and would like to consolidate the accounts.

It is possible to transfer an inherited IRA from one custodian to another; however, few financial institutions handle this process competently. It is very easy to create a taxable event or even lose the tax benefits of the inherited stretch IRA altogether if the transfer is mishandled. If you wish to transfer custodians, consult a qualified tax advisor who can oversee the process.

Avoid inherited IRA tax penalties. As with a contributory IRA where a mandatory annual distribution must take place, the inherited stretch IRA also requires that a minimum distribution take place for both Roth and non-Roth inherited IRAs. It is not the responsibility of the financial institution to make sure the correct amount is distributed; it is the responsibility of the inherited IRA beneficiary.

Note: *The tax penalty for failing to take this minimum distribution is 50% of the undistributed amount.*

Forgetting to take the RMD. Often the distractions of everyday life will cause an IRA owner to forget to take the required minimum distribution. To ensure that this never happens to you, set up your inherited stretch IRA with a custodian who automatically withdraws the proper amount each year. This distribution must be made by December 31 each year.

Timely account segregation. The accounts must be split into segregated accounts for each individual beneficiary before any beneficiary takes a distribution. If this does not occur before any distributions are made, all the beneficiaries will have to use the age of the oldest beneficiary to determine their required minimum distributions.

Also, if a charity is a beneficiary and the accounts are not segregated at the time of the distribution, all of the beneficiaries will lose the chance to receive their tax-deferred inheritance as a stretch IRA. The time following the death of a loved one can be emotional. Anxiety and lack of focus can cause a substantial loss of wealth. Be sure to see your tax or legal advisor before making any distributions.

Beneficiaries forget to name a beneficiary. After the IRA has been inherited, a beneficiary must be named so if the person who inherited the IRA dies, it can be passed on to their heirs and avoid probate. This is a common mistake since most financial institutions will not tell you this, nor do they typically have any beneficiary designation forms readily available for this situation.

Get professional assistance!

As you can see, there are many things to consider when it comes to IRA planning. In my opinion, you cannot learn everything that needs to be considered. The reason is because the rules are always changing. While I encourage everyone to have a clear understanding of their finances and these types of accounts, you will either need to have some professional assistance or make the decision to spend the time and effort required to become your own specialist. As a professional in this field, I can tell you that it takes many hours and continuing effort to keep up. The amount of help you need will be determined by your goals. If you consider using professional help, look for financial planners that specialize in this area. While this may seem like a lot of effort, the payoff could be well worth it for both you and your heirs.

Chapter 2

Creating a Structured Income Plan

Imagine you have retired and that you live longer than you ever thought you would. Prices are rising but you don't want to risk your investments to keep up. Many today are beginning to see this as a reality. The financial threats that American retirees face now are different from any time before. The retirement years of today's retiree will be unlike any time previously experienced. It is essential to be prepared.

Let me explain some of the reasons behind these massive changes. In 1900, the average life expectancy of a male was age 46. This means a 40-year-old would have been considered old. By the time Social Security was introduced in

1936, life expectancy had increased to age 63. Today, a married couple aged 65 has a 40% probability for one of them to live to age 95.

Our world is rapidly changing and advancements occur at a fast pace. These changes affect our life expectancy and quality of life. Just think of the advancements that have occurred in the last 100 years. Today, someone in their 40s is considered to be in the prime of life. In contrast to the year 1900, today's 70-year-old resembles the then 40-year-old. Retirements that last 30 or 40 years are becoming commonplace. As retirements grow lengthier, one of the great challenges retirees face is making their income last the entire time. As prices continue to rise, inflation creates another challenge.

Historically, between Social Security from the government and corporate pensions from employers, individuals used to have up to 2/3 of their retirement income guaranteed. Today's soon-to-be retirees and those currently retired live in a very different world.

Social Security is in the news constantly with threats that massive changes to that system will have to occur. In fact, on the front page of your Social Security statement it says, "In 2016 we will begin paying more in benefits than we collect in taxes. Without changes, by 2037 the Social Security Trust Fund will be exhausted and there will be enough money to pay only about 76 cents for each dollar of scheduled benefits."

What about corporations? Most corporations have discontinued pension plans and replaced them with defined contribution plans, shifting responsibility to individuals. What is the result? Retirees can only expect that about 1/3 of their retirement income will be guaranteed. More than ever, a plan for structured income is needed to achieve security in retirement.

There are different opinions on how to approach this issue. I would like to share with you a common sense approach to solving this challenge, an approach with a core objective to provide reliable, inflation-adjusted income that will last for life.

Let's first talk about one of the challenges investors are confronted with. Investors struggle with having to stay invested in the stock market during downturns. We know the goal is to buy low and sell while the market is higher. When markets fluctuate, our emotions, fears, and concerns about outliving our income kick in and many buy high or sell when the market is low. Often, the result is that many end up with returns much lower than the overall market, even losing the value of their retirement funds. The approach I will discuss focuses on the amount of time you can be in the market. While in the past most investors have focused on R.O.I. (return on investment), I propose a new definition of R.O.I.: reliability of income. Creating a reliable, inflation-adjusted income is the focus of this approach.

To start, let's project a 25-year period and divide it into five equal segments. Each segment will account for

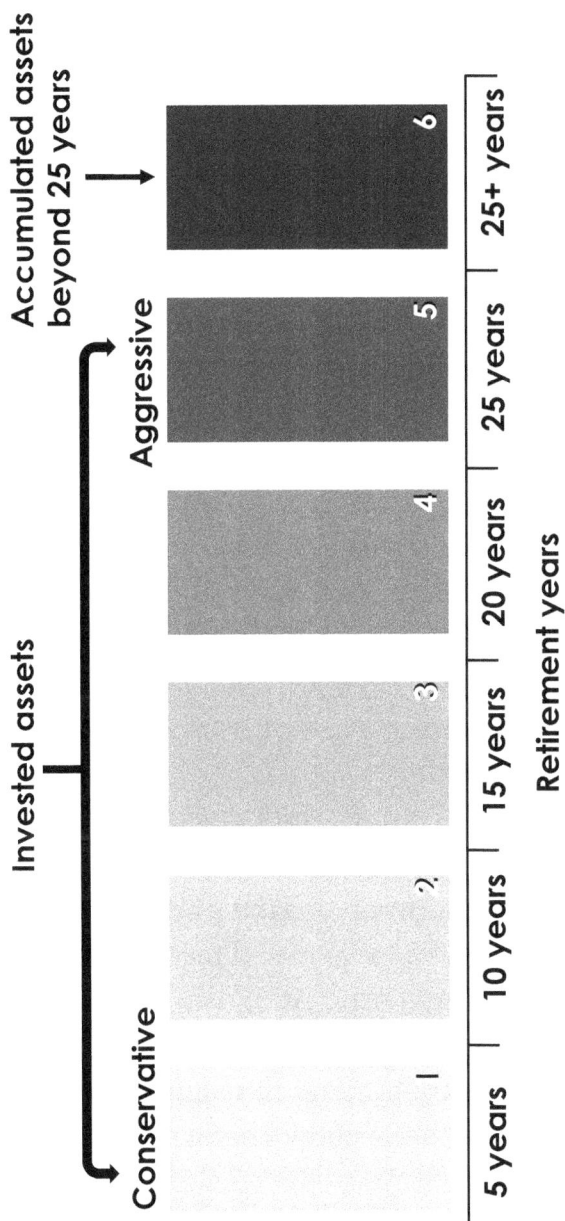

Accumulated assets beyond 25 years

Invested assets

Aggressive

Conservative

| 1 | 2 | 3 | 4 | 5 | 6 |

| 5 years | 10 years | 15 years | 20 years | 25 years | 25+ years |

Retirement years

5 years. In segments 1-5, investments will range from conservative to aggressive. For this same projection, we will also add in a sixth segment, the goal of which is to accumulate assets beyond 25 years. The more aggressive investments will be held in segments that will allow for the longest time periods in the market. Research has indicated that the risk of volatility increases as investment classes became more aggressive. Higher rates of return have been historically associated with higher volatility and risk of loss. History also indicates the probability of more aggressive investment classes achieving higher rates of return increased over time.

We all know that past performance is not a guarantee of future results. All investing involves risk and you may incur a profit or a loss. The more aggressive an investment is the more risk it is subject to. Let's look at the research done by Ibbotson® that measures actual investment class performance. Looking over a 50-year period we can see how this works. We will associate each class to one of our six segments.

- Segment one (years 1–5): One-year treasury bills have averaged 5.3%*

- Segment two (years 6–10): Intermediate government bonds held for 5-year periods have averaged 7.26%*

- Segment three (years 11–15): The S&P 500 Composite Stock Index held for 10-year periods has averaged 10.58%*

- Segment four (years 16–20): Large cap stocks held for 15-year periods have averaged 11.18%*

- Segment five (years 21–25): Small cap stocks held for 20-year periods have averaged 14.78%*

- Segment six (year 26 and beyond): Small cap stocks held for 25-year periods have averaged 14.91%*

*These are historical growth rates of return not inclusive of any investment expenses or fees. To take into account today's current economic climate, rates of return will be reduced considerably for examples or illustrations.

In order to build an example, we will need to make some assumptions. Let's consider how each segment can be funded. These vehicles are suggestions based on my opinions and experience.

- Segment one: Immediate income annuity, laddered CD portfolio, and other fixed vehicles. The key for this segment is to provide guaranteed monthly income.

- Segment two: Short-term bond, fixed annuity contract

- Segment three: Investments subject to stock market risk

- Segments four, five, and six: Investment vehicles offering more aggressive growth portfolios (the more aggressive an investment, the more risk it is subject to)

An important phase in creating a structured income plan is identifying your income needs. It is important in this step to separate income into different categories. Your income plan will need to have an income floor. The income floor will take care of your income needs (category one). The income floor should be income that you don't have to worry about losing or that requires a specific rate of return. I have listed the three essential categories below.

Category one: Income needs

The income for category one is for your essential needs. Think of the things you will need on either a monthly or annual basis. These would be things like food, clothing, insurance, mortgage/rent, property taxes, utilities, etc. In this category, make sure you limit it to the essentials. This category is the basis for the creation of your income floor. The income floor is the minimum income you will need each month for your entire retirement.

Category two: Income wants

In category two, include the extras you may want. You may include things like vacations, new cars, or home upgrades. Maybe you like to pamper yourself with spa treatments or you like to treat others to dinner. As you think about this category, include any wants. You do not need them to live, but they make your life more comfortable. Also, for this category, consider the phases of retirement. Phase one will be the part of retirement in which you likely will be the most active and do more, thus requiring additional income. In phase one you may have more wants than when you get into the later phase of retirement when you are not as active. Perhaps you will need additional income for wants during the first 10 or 15 years. Then, in the later years of retirement, those wants may not be there.

Category three: Income gifting

Category three is your plan for gifting. This may include things like assisting a grandchild with college or charitable donations. Maybe you want to help your children by gifting them money now instead of waiting for them to inherit it. From time to time, I have clients who say they would like to see the joy or benefit from the gifts and not wait until they die to give certain funds to their beneficiaries. Your plan for this category is obviously a personal choice.

Income plan illustrated

Now that we have thought through the needs, wants, and gifts, let's consider an example. John and Mary are six months from the day they have looked forward to for years: their retirement! As they have thought through the categories of income, they have concluded that their income needs are $3,800 per month. For wants, they would like to budget $15,000 per year or $1,250 per month. John and Mary would like to gift some funds for their two grandchildren's college education in the amount of $500 per month. In order for all category goals to be achieved, the total income needed is $5,550 per month. It is important to note that this is after tax. They will need to figure income taxes on top of this. For this example, we will assume they are in a 25% tax bracket. This means they will need gross income of $6,938 each month to net $5,550 after paying taxes.

John and Mary have assets from retirement accounts, savings, and fixed income listed below:

Investable assets
John's 401(k) $525,000
Mary's 401(k)..........................$240,000
Roth IRA accounts combined...$62,000
Brokerage account $250,000
Savings in CDs/
Money Markets $70,000
Total investable assets .. $1,147,000

Fixed income
John's Social Security $1,500/month
Mary's Social Security ... $1,000/month
Mary's pension $1,000/month
Total fixed income.... $3,500/month

We now know their income needs, wants, and gifts, as well as their current assets and fixed income. Remember for their category one income needs, John and Mary needed a net income of $3,800 per month. If we add income tax to this, they will need gross dollars of about $4,750 per month. This means for their needs, they need an additional $1,250 per month ($4,750 needed - $3,500 fixed income = $1,250).

There are key points to consider when choosing the type of financial vehicle to produce the $1,250 per month.

- The amount of income needs to be guaranteed.

- The income should not be determined based on the rate of return of the underlying investment.

- The length of time the income lasts from the financial vehicle should be for their lifetime.

At this point, John and Mary will need some assistance. I recommend contacting a financial planner that specializes in retirement planning and works on a fiduciary basis. (See Chapter 6 for further explanation.) One option that could work for John and Mary is an annuity with an attached rider that guarantees an income stream for life. In the world of annuities, there are many options. You must be careful to fully consider fees and terms before signing an annuity contract. The advantage to an annuity is that it can be a source of guaranteed income (the guarantee is subject to the financial strength and claims-paying ability of the issuing insurance company). It would be advisable to consult a fee-based financial advisor who can give you unbiased information about the pros and cons of the annuities you are considering. Annuities can have high fees and surrender charges. Some insurance companies are creating options today for individuals to obtain annuities with much lower fees and no surrender charges. There are many varieties and constant changes occurring with annuities and annuity providers. You will want to do thorough research before purchasing.

For the purposes of illustration, suppose John and Mary could find an annuity that would payout 5.5% of the balance and guarantee this for life. In order for them to receive the $1,250 per month to fulfill their income floor, they would need to place approximately $272,728 in the annuity. They would receive $15,000 per year or $1,250 per month on 5.5% of $272,728. (Please keep in mind, this example is not product- or company-specific and may not be a good choice for your particular situation.) A rider on the annuity contract could allow for a specific percentage of the balance to be paid and, regardless of the performance of the initial amount put into the annuity, continue to pay out the income for life.

Once John and Mary have chosen a financial vehicle to provide the $1,250 per month, they can now move on to considering how to fund the remaining segments of the structured income plan. As they consider how to fund the other segments, they can feel at ease knowing that their basic income needs are taken care of. This is a major step in achieving a worry-free retirement. Just think of what this step will have accomplished! Regardless of the market or rates of return, their basic income needs will not be affected. The income floor is fixed. They can go to sleep each night without worrying about news of a deteriorating economy. Now they have the freedom to focus on what they may feel are the more important things—the things in life not associated with finances. If you develop your own structured income plan like John and Mary have—one that fits your own needs and situation—you could have the same worry-free retirement.

Each of the segments have a job. Segments one, two, and three will provide additional income for the wants and gifting desires. When funding these segments, it is important to remember the income desired is immediate. You would not want to take very high risk in these segments, because risky investments could erase principal due to a stock market decline. The goal is to take the emotional rollercoaster out of the income plan. Remember, most retirees in the past have kept their retirement accounts invested in risky investments. Due to this, when the market declines, they feel it necessary to stop taking income. This action adds to their anxiety and reduces their income.

Just imagine your retirement income plan not being jeopardized by a decline in the stock market. A well-thought-out and structured income plan is one step that can add enormous peace of mind in retirement. In the past, most have rationalized that they must take extra risk in order not to forfeit future growth. As you think through this, you will see that is not the case. You will still have other segments invested for future growth. You will also realize that you are achieving R.O.I. as we have re-defined it—reliability of income. With the first three segments, this reliability of income is more important in retirement years than the return on investment.

Segments four through six will be invested with longer time horizons with the goal of providing growth for future inflation and income needs. In these segments, there could be balance fluctuations from time to time. That is not as worrisome because the goals for these segments are different. In these segments, you do not need immediate income. Therefore, if the market declines, the anxiety you would have normally had will be greatly reduced. You will not worry about your income needs and feel forced to sell your investments at the wrong time. You will have more confidence to stay invested for the longer term. Studies have shown that, in most cases, the longer you stay invested the greater chance you have to make a positive return. While no one likes to see their balances go down, you can look at it in a different way for these segments. Most retirees correlate their balance to their income, but with this income plan you can change the viewpoint. The two are not attached. Your income will continue and your basic needs will be taken care of.

When discussing this structured income plan, I have purposefully kept this to a big picture view. Each situation will vary. The specifics of your income plan will need to be personal. The way the plan is specifically structured will differ based on your income needs and assets. If you want to see how your plan would look, you now have an outline on which to build lifetime income.

Plan review

It is important to understand that there is a need to closely monitor the plan. If you work with an advisor, this would be something you do together. I recommend getting at least a quarterly update with a more extensive review done annually. I like to think of the client as the CEO (Chief Executive Officer) of their retirement plan and the advisor as the CFO (Chief Financial Officer). This means you are the boss and you call the shots. The advisor explains and monitors the plan, reporting the results to you. As the CEO, you have responsibilities. Make sure you completely understand the income plan and any investments recommended. Do your own research and ask lots of questions. Your advisor should be patient and answer your questions in detail. You want to completely understand exactly how your advisor will get paid and if there are conflicts of interest with their recommendations. By following these steps, you can have peace of mind that allows you to have a purposeful and fulfilling retirement.

Income Plan Illustration

Income Floor $227,273 Total Investment: $953,158

Year Starting	Income from Segments	Total	Segment 1 14.71% 1.00%	Segment 2 15.55% 4.00%	Segment 3 13.81% 6.00%	Segment 4 11.43% 7.00%	Segment 5 8.49% 8.00%	Segment 6 12.17% 9.00%	Total
		Net Growth Rate of Return							
1	2396	6920	$ 140,188	$ 148,258	$ 131,605	$ 108,981	$ 80,885	$ 115,968	$ 953,158
2	2396	6988	$ -	$ 154,189	$ 139,501	$ 116,609	$ 87,356	$ 126,405	$ 624,060
3	2396	7039	$ -	$ 160,356	$ 147,871	$ 124,772	$ 34,345	$ 137,781	$ 605,125
4	2396	7091	$ -	$ 166,770	$ 156,774	$ 133,506	$ 101,892	$ 150,182	$ 709,124
5	2396	7144	$ -	$ 173,441	$ 166,148	$ 142,851	$ 110,044	$ 163,698	$ 756,182
6	3241	8043	$ -	$ 180,379	$ 176,117	$ 152,851	$ 118,847	$ 178,431	$ 806,625
7	3241	8098	$ -	$ -	$ 186,684	$ 163,550	$ 128,355	$ 194,490	$ 673,079
8	3241	8154	$ -	$ -	$ 197,885	$ 174,999	$ 138,623	$ 211,994	$ 723,501
9	3241	8212	$ -	$ -	$ 209,758	$ 187,249	$ 149,713	$ 231,073	$ 777,793
10	3241	8270	$ -	$ -	$ 222,344	$ 200,356	$ 161,690	$ 251,870	$ 836,260
11	4235	9324	$ -	$ -	$ 235,684	$ 214,381	$ 174,626	$ 274,538	$ 899,229
12	4235	9385	$ -	$ -	$ -	$ 229,388	$ 188,596	$ 299,246	$ 717,230
13	4235	9447	$ -	$ -	$ -	$ 245,445	$ 203,683	$ 326,179	$ 775,307
14	4235	9511	$ -	$ -	$ -	$ 262,626	$ 219,978	$ 355,535	$ 838,139
15	4235	9575	$ -	$ -	$ -	$ 281,010	$ 237,576	$ 387,533	$ 906,119
16	5403	10809	$ -	$ -	$ -	$ 300,681	$ 256,582	$ 422,411	$ 979,674
17	5403	10877	$ -	$ -	$ -	$ -	$ 377,109	$ 460,428	$ 837,537
18	5403	10945	$ -	$ -	$ -	$ -	$ 299,278	$ 501,866	$ 801,144
19	5403	11015	$ -	$ -	$ -	$ -	$ 323,220	$ 547,034	$ 870,254
20	5403	11087	$ -	$ -	$ -	$ -	$ 249,077	$ 596,267	$ 845,344
21	6774	12531	$ -	$ -	$ -	$ -	$ 377,004	$ 649,931	$ 1,026,935
22	6774	12605	$ -	$ -	$ -	$ -	$ -	$ 708,425	$ 708,425
23	6774	12681	$ -	$ -	$ -	$ -	$ -	$ 772,184	$ 772,184
24	6774	12758	$ -	$ -	$ -	$ -	$ -	$ 841,680	$ 841,680
25	6774	12837	$ -	$ -	$ -	$ -	$ -	$ 917,431	$ 917,431
			$ -	$ -	$ -	$ -	$ -	$ 1,000,000	$ 1,000,000

Summary: $953,158 Total Investment: $1,635,471 Ending Balance: $1,000,000

This is a hypothetical example for illustrative purposes only. It is not intended to reflect the actual performance of any security. Investments involve risk and you may incur a profit or a loss. Calculated monthly payments are subject to the financial strength and claims-paying ability of the issuing insurance company.
*The rate of return used in this projection is hypothetical and does not reflect the performance of any individual investment or group of investments. The returns do not reflect the reinvestment of dividends or other distributions. The returns also do not reflect the deduction of any taxes, which will lower the stated returns. An investment's return will fluctuate over time, and may experience times of negative growth. There is no guarantee that over the time period shown, your account will achieve the projected return. Investing involves risk, including loss of principal. An investor's shares, when sold, may be worth more or less than the original purchase price. Past performance does not guarantee future results. Withdrawing more or less than the amounts shown will affect the stated returns.

Segment Allocation

One goal of the model is to place smaller amounts of money in more aggressive assets. The more aggressive an investment, the more risk it is subject to. Risk investments will be held for the longest period of time in order to achieve the best possible chance of attaining rate-of-return objectives.

Risk

Conservative   Aggressive

$148,258

$140,188

$131,605

$115,968

$108,981

$80,885

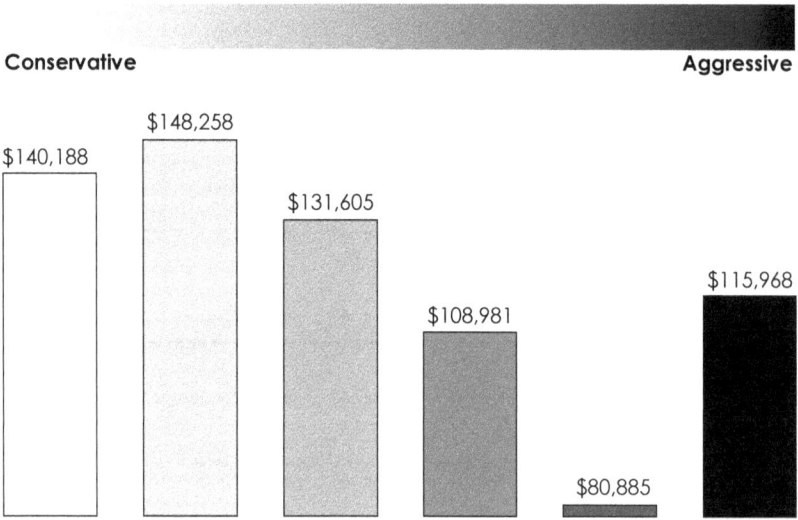

	Allocation Percentage	Investment Amount	Income Provided
Segment 1	14.71%	$140,188	Years 1–5
Segment 2	15.55%	$148,258	Years 6–10
Segment 3	13.81%	$131,605	Years 11–15
Segment 4	11.43%	$108,981	Years 16–20
Segment 5	8.49%	$80,885	Years 21–25
Investment Segment	12.17%	$115,968	Years 25+
Allocation to Income Floor	23.84%	$227,273	Years 1–Lifetime

Creating a Structured Income Plan

The following table illustrates the allocation of $953,157.20 into distinct segments. Each segment will provide income for a specific period. A segment may consist of a period in which it grows at an assumed rate of return and also a period in which it is liquidated to produce income.

	Allocation Percentage	Rate of Return Assumption	Total Duration
Segment 1	14.71%	1%	5 years
Segment 2	15.55%	4%	10 years
Segment 3	13.81%	6%	15 years
Segment 4	11.43%	7%	20 years
Segment 5	8.49%	8%	25 years
Investment Segment	12.17%	9%	25+ years
Allocation to Income Floor	23.84%	0%	Lifetime

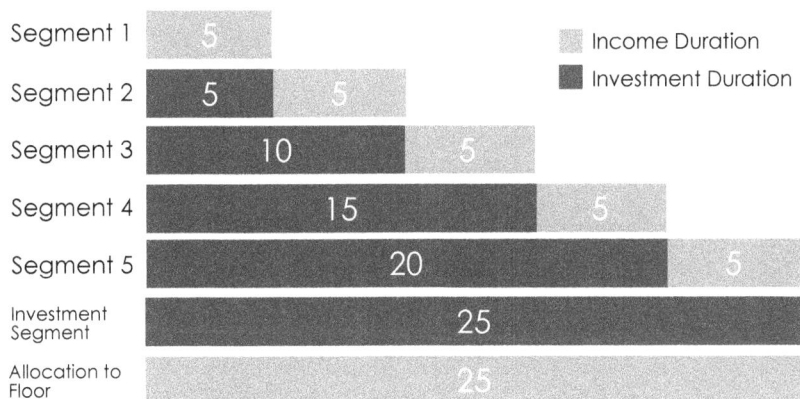

*The rates of return shown are hypothetical and are not intended to reflect the actual performance of any security. Investing involves risk and you may incur a profit or a loss. Investments with higher rates of return are associated with higher volatility and greater risk of loss. There is no guarantee that any or all segments will obtain their desired results. If desired returns are not met in any investment segment, this could cause the investor to run out of income before the end of that income segment. To continue drawing income, the investor may have to remove funds from other investment segments before scheduled. This action could lead to additional fees and ultimately the failure of the plan to meet the original objectives. Investors may have to adjust their income amounts to compensate for any investment segment not meeting its goal in order for the actual cash value to last the duration of that income segment.

Chapter 3

A Basic Understanding of the Economy

One of the biggest questions on the minds of retirees is, "Where is the economy headed?" There is good reason to ask this question. If you are thinking of retiring or have already retired, the economy could determine if your retirement will be prosperous or not. Of course, I am speaking about finances and not the most important things like family, friends, health, and spiritual well-being.

For many, economic concerns impact their peace of mind. Just go on the Internet and Google "where is the economy headed." Over 20 million results come up. If you read articles written by economists, you may feel more confused than before you started your research. Some say the U.S. economy is going to expand and others say our economy is in store for a great retraction. How can we use logical reasoning and not get caught up in exhaustive numbers and opinions? I would like to share with you some things that help me and my clients to reasonably understand how our economy is fed and to understand if we will see an economic expansion or retraction. This provides a big picture view. What we are about to discuss does not reveal how the stock market is going to react in the next month. Rather, it gives an overview of how things might begin to look in the coming years.

What makes up the U.S. economy?

Let's start with the basics. The measure used to determine the U.S. economy is Gross Domestic Product or GDP. What makes up GDP? GDP = personal consumption + gross investment + government spending + (exports – imports). The part of GDP that I want to focus on is personal consumption. The reason I think we should focus here is because it is the largest part of GDP. It equates to more than 70% of GDP.

In general terms, personal consumption is what individuals spend their money on. For example, it includes what we spend on food, clothing, housing, recreation, services, health care, and transportation. If you look at the chart, you will see that from 1982 to 2008, personal consumption increased year after year. Note that there was a decrease in spending in 2009. It is very important to understand why this

U.S. Personal Consumption 1982–2009

■ Spending in billions

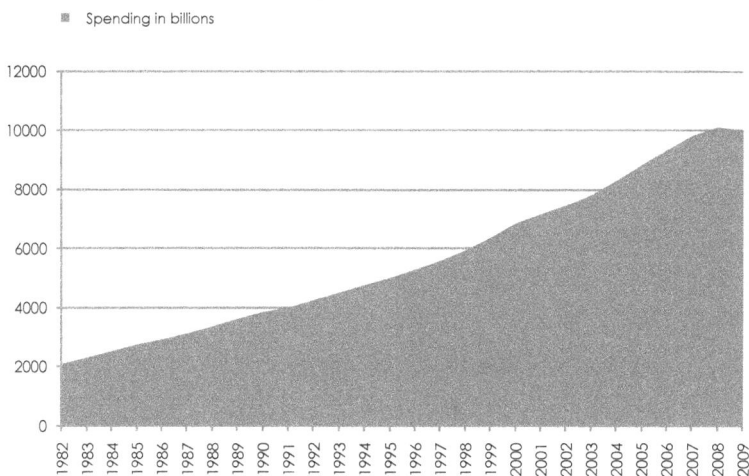

happened. The first reaction someone may have when seeing this decline is to dismiss it due to our recent economic turmoil. There was a major decline in the stock market, right? A drop in personal consumption makes sense, right? Think back to 2001 and 2002. The U.S. stock market had a major decline, there was a terrorist attack in the U.S., and the war against terrorism started! Why was there not a decline in personal consumption then?

If personal consumption is responsible for more than 70% of the U.S. economy, then it is important to analyze it further. Fluctuations in personal consumption will likely make the U.S. economy expand or contract. If this is true, then we need to consider whether consumer spending will be more or less. To do this, we need to look at the spending habits of families and determine when they spend the most. What is the period of life when people spend the most money? Statistically, people spend the most from ages 45–54. Why? That's when child-related expenses are highest. College is being paid for, and cars and other large ticket items are being purchased. The next step in the analysis is to look at the U.S. population and demographics. Baby boomers make up one of the largest segments of the U.S. population. The United States Census Bureau considers a baby boomer to be someone born between 1946 and 1964. There are an estimated 78 million U.S. baby boomers.

Let's look at how this massive number of people impact the economy. Think about the big economic boom that started in the '90s. Correlate that to the baby boomer generation. The oldest of the group started turning 45 years old in 1991 at an amazing rate of approximately 10,000 people per day. They entered the biggest spending phase of their life and the economy picked up steam. They were putting kids in college, buying bigger homes, and purchasing large ticket items. This continued until they started entering the next phase of life.

The oldest of this group will be turning 65 in 2011. A majority of baby boomers have lived through their biggest spending years. An estimated 37,000,000 baby boomers are now in the next phase of life. Think about yourself, your neighbors, and your friends. What is the next financial goal after the kids are out of school and you are 55 years old or older? Retirement! You are now in the savings phase of life preparing for retirement. Is there any kind of government stimulus that will motivate you to increase spending? No! You are saving everything. You want to retire and you have only a few years to get ready. This is one of the main reasons we have started to see declines in consumer spending. This trend will continue as the remaining baby boomers enter the savings phase. It only makes sense that the economy will slow as consumer demand declines. This, in turn, will affect stock prices. We likely will see unemployment remain high and perhaps get even worse for a while.

There is a bright side to this story. We have a very large generation being created right now known as Generation Y, also referred to as Echo Boomers. They are around 60 million strong and will eventually create economic growth again. It will take a few years before that cycle happens.

It is interesting to note that this same type of cycle occurred with the Japanese economy in the early '90s. Japan's equivalent of the U.S. baby boom generation is older. Japan's baby boomers moved into their spending phase in the '70s. Japan was the economic example for many other countries at the time. In the '70s and '80s their economy boomed. The Japanese Nikkei 225 (similar to the U.S. Dow Jones) skyrocketed from 10,000 in 1984 to nearly 40,000 in early 1990. Then this generation began to peak in number and entered their savings phase of life. What do you think happened? Their economy started to slow down. Consider that in 1995 the Nikkei 225 was at 20,000. By 2001, it had fallen to 10,000. That's a

75% drop in value from the peak. In the same timeframe, home values fell drastically.

Everyone knows that when the economy starts to slow down, all that is needed is a government stimulus, right? Japan tried this. They pumped the equivalent of hundreds of billions of dollars into their economy in the '90s and lowered interest rates to nearly 0%. Do you think it worked? You're right, it did not. Many of their consumers had entered into a phase of life for saving. Nothing the government did encouraged them to spend more. A major difference between Japan and the U.S. is their population growth. Japan had discouraged family growth and did not have a new generation sufficiently large enough to grow their economy. They still have not fully recovered from this economic cycle.

As we focus on the U.S. economy and consider our demographics, it is reasonable to assume we are in for a few years of slow, declining economic conditions. Does this mean that you should not invest for growth? Not exactly. It means you need to have a plan that takes the overall situation into account. From 1985 to 2007, the "buy and hold" mantra was born. Most came to realize after the major stock market declines of 2001, 2002, 2008, and the beginning of 2009 that mantra should die. In the current investing environment, flexibility is crucial.

If you have created an income plan and are considering how to invest your funds, you will want to look at it differently than you have in the past. What is the right way to invest? There is not only one right way. As you talk to financial advisors, ask them what their opinions are about the economy and the stock market. If they do not have an opinion or give you broad, sweeping statements, I would encourage you to look somewhere else for an advisor. You want someone who considers many aspects of the economy and is specific in their investing approach. Do not use an advisor who gives a random 60% stocks/40% bonds allocation and tells you to "hang in there" when things start to fall.

I hope this has given you a basic overview of the U.S. economy. I don't mean this to sound like doom and gloom. I think as people are educated about the economy, they can plan better. There are people that did not lose much in the downturns of 2001, 2002, 2008 and 2009. Why? They made changes. They were able to see things the majority of others didn't. I hope this allows you to see some things you did not see earlier and it helps you to weather any future downturns.

Chapter 4

Understanding Annuities

When you hear the word "annuity" what comes to your mind? I would guess that whatever thoughts come to you, they are most likely negative ones. Maybe you personally had a bad experience with an insurance company. Possibly you know someone, either a family member or friend, who has told you about their experience. The media has exposed some of the negative aspects of these investments through hidden camera news specials. Given all this, I think there is good reason for people to have negative feelings about annuities.

In my experience, the majority of negative situations surrounding annuities tend not to be about the product sold, but rather the salesperson behind the transaction. Many have been caught either telling direct lies or stretching the facts to sound better than the actual truth. Sometimes the salespeople did not lie, but knew the product was not appropriate for the person they were selling it to. At the same time, there are many people who are completely satisfied with their annuity. Many praise the fact that they have income they cannot outlive. Others say how happy they are that their money is earning an attractive interest rate and they lost nothing when the stock market fell. Some will tell you they were excited that they had purchased an annuity that allowed them to invest in the stock market while still providing a guaranteed income stream protected against losses.

The purpose of this chapter is not to make you for or against annuities. The fact is that billions of dollars are invested in annuities each year. Many of my current and prospective clients ask me about annuities and how they work. Many complain that they have a hard time trusting salespeople. They know their objective is to sell a product and they fear the salesperson will say anything to get a sale.

In this chapter, I will share with you the basics of annuities, the different ways they can be set up, and the positive and negative things you should be aware of.

First of all, what is an annuity?

Typically purchased from an insurance company, an annuity is an investment vehicle. Normally, it is used to secure retirement income and pays a fixed number of payments over a set time period. The annuity represents a contract between you and the insurance company. The specifics of the annuity are outlined in the contract. The details vary depending on the type of annuity chosen.

There are three ways to categorize an annuity:

1. Is it fixed rate or variable? This determines how money is invested in the annuity.

2. Do you want income now or later? This establishes if the income is deferred or immediate.

3. Is the annuity single premium or flexible? This determines if additional funds can be added to the investment.

There are four parties to an annuity.

The insurer. An annuity is always an agreement between you and an insurance company. This applies even if you buy the annuity from an independent agent, a bank, or directly from the insurance company. Your money is invested according to your instructions and the type of annuity (fixed rate or variable, immediate or deferred). The insurer is governed by the details of the contract, which outlines what can and cannot be done with the investment. The contract spells out guarantees, cancellation penalties, as well as rules governing deposits and withdrawals.

The contract owner. The contract owner is the individual who has invested in the annuity; they are the entity that provides the money for the investment. The owner chooses which options are utilized. They may add funds to the investment, terminate the agreement, or withdraw some or all of the money. The owner can change beneficiaries as well as the ownership named in the contract. Individuals, couples, partnerships, corporations, or trusts may legally be a contract owner. The owner can gift or will part or all of the contract to any individual or entity they choose.

The annuitant. This part of the contract can be one of the most confusing. The annuitant can be the contract owner, but does not have to be. Think of the annuitant in terms of life insurance. With life insurance, if the person who is insured dies, then the contract terminates. With an annuity, the annuitant is the measuring life of the contract. An annuitant is the person during whose life an annuity is payable. Until the contract owner makes a change or the person named as annuitant dies, the terms of the annuity remain in force. The annuitant, then, is like the insured in a life insurance policy. The annuitant can be anyone: you, a spouse, parent, child, or other relative. The annuitant must be an individual, so it cannot be a trust, corporation, or partnership.

The beneficiary. The beneficiary of an annuity is similar to beneficiaries of other investments. Upon the annuitant's death, the beneficiary receives the inheritance. The beneficiary cannot change or control the contract. He or she has no say in how funds are invested. The beneficiary only benefits from an annuity upon the annuitant's death. A beneficiary can be a child, spouse, friend, relative, trust, corporation, or partnership. An annuity can have multiple beneficiaries with varying percentages payable to each equaling 100%. The contract owner can change beneficiaries at any time and the consent of a beneficiary is not necessary for changes to be made.

Types of annuities

Annuities can be split into two main categories: immediate and deferred. A deciding factor for choosing the annuity type you want will be based on your income needs and the flexibility desired. Do you want income now or in a few years? Do you want access to a lump sum of money? Would you like the largest possible income? These are just a few of the questions you would need to think through before purchasing an annuity.

Immediate annuity

If you purchase an immediate annuity you are trading a lump sum of money for an income stream. For example, you may give an insurance company $100,000 in return for $500 per month for the rest of your life regardless of how long you live. The amount of income would be based on your age and possibly your health. You also could have payments sent to you for a specified number of years. The amount of income would be based on interest rates and the number of years you want income. In any case, you can have the checks sent to you monthly, quarterly, semi-annually, or annually.

Many of my clients and potential clients do not like this type of annuity because they feel they lose too much control. Once you have traded your lump sum of money for an income stream, the insurance company does not allow access to the remaining funds.

Deferred annuity

Most people purchase an annuity to grow their money. The majority of people will never turn these funds into a lifetime income stream. The flexibility of deferred annuities, whether fixed or variable, is the main attraction. Deferred annuities offer guarantees for income planning, but the contract owner can decide to start or stop the income stream at any time. The contract could allow the money to simply grow without withdrawals or allow the owner to take interest earned or withdraw the principal.

With deferred annuities, there are three ways to grow the money. You can purchase a fixed rate, fixed index, or variable annuity. These types of annuities can be set up for a short or long period of time. The earnings in the account can be taken out or automatically reinvested for future growth.

With most deferred annuities, there is a period of time during which the funds can be subject to surrender charges. The charges are incurred only if funds are withdrawn in excess of the free withdrawal percentage. Most annuities allow the owner to withdraw up to 10% each year without incurring a surrender charge. The surrender charge period is stated in the contract and is typically five to ten years. The surrender charge gradually decreases to zero over the specified period. There are some annuities available that have no surrender charges.

Deferred annuity investment types

As was stated earlier, there are three ways for the money to be invested in a deferred annuity: fixed rate, fixed index, and variable. Let's look at the basics of each.

Fixed rate annuities

Like other fixed rate products, a fixed rate annuity provides the contract owner with a guaranteed rate of return. These are similar to bank CDs (although CDs are FDIC-insured, while annuities are not). When you purchase a CD from a bank, the interest you receive usually depends on the time commitment; the longer the commitment, the higher the interest rate. A fixed rate annuity operates in a similar way. Just like banks, some insurance companies offer higher rates than others.

The most common time horizons for fixed rate annuities are one, three, or five years. When you invest in a CD, the interest rate is locked in for a specified time. The same is true with a fixed rate annuity. The interest the annuity earns can be sent to the contract owner or reinvested to take advantage of compound interest.

Fixed rate annuities are popular for individuals who want to keep their principal safe. With this type of annuity, you will know exactly what to expect each year in interest. Fixed rate annuities work great for conservative investors or those who want to know exactly what they will have earned at the end of a specific timeframe.

Fixed index annuities

Fixed index annuities are a hybrid product. They combine the safety of principal offered by a fixed rate annuity with interest earnings linked to a market index (such as the S&P 500, Dow Jones, NASDAQ, Russell 2000, EURO STOXX 50, etc.). Fixed index annuities have been offered in the U.S. since the mid-1990s. They have all the features of most fixed rate annuity contracts except that the interest earned is determined by the performance of the index to which the annuity is linked.

Most fixed index annuities use multiple formulas to calculate the interest to be credited. A popular crediting method is the annual point to point with an interest cap. "Annual point to point" is based on the contract anniversary each year, there being two points each year—one at the beginning and another at the end. The interest cap is the maximum you can earn in a given year. For example, suppose you invested $100,000 and the interest crediting was linked to the S&P 500. Suppose the S&P 500 on the date you purchased the annuity (the first point) was valued at 1,000. One year later (the second point) on your contract anniversary, the S&P 500 is valued at 1,100. By doing some simple math you will find that the index has gained 10%. Let's assume the interest cap is 6%. The interest credited to your account will be 6% of $100,000, or $6,000, making your account balance $106,000. This amount becomes your base and your account can never go below $106,000 unless you withdraw funds. Even if the index declines the following year, your base is protected. The worst you can do in a year is make 0%. This protection is why fixed index annuities have been popular with investors.

One main detraction of fixed index annuities is their complication. There are several methods for calculating interest. This has steered many away from using them. My recommendation is that if you decide to use a fixed index annuity, choose one that is easy for you to understand. Make sure the advisor you are working with explains everything in detail and supports in writing their answers to any questions you may have.

Variable annuities

For individuals who have a higher risk tolerance, variable annuities offer an alternative. When you invest in a variable annuity, you control how your funds are invested in the annuity. Under the umbrella of a tax-deferred annuity there are usually many types of mutual funds in which to invest. The contract owner can allocate their money from mutual fund to mutual fund. (Some annuity contracts limit the frequency of movements.) With a variable annuity, you typically are investing in the stock market or bonds; therefore, there is risk of loss. If the investment does well, you receive all the benefit minus any fees. If the investment performs poorly, you can lose gains and even principal. There are several fees associated with a variable annuity. Most have mortality expenses, mutual fund, and surrender fees. These fees can vary from one annuity to another and can be very costly. These fees can come as a big surprise if you are unaware of how they are charged.

Income and death benefit riders

Some insurance companies allow a contract owner to attach different riders to an annuity at the time of purchase. Most riders come with annual fees. A popular rider is a death benefit rider. These come in different forms based on the contract. Some insure the principal at the death of the annuitant regardless of market declines. For example, suppose you invested $100,000.

Due to market declines, the value had dropped to $75,000 at the time of death of the annuitant. The death benefit rider would pay the beneficiary the amount invested ($100,000) minus any prior withdrawals. There are also versions of the death benefit rider that guarantee an actual growth rate on the initial investment.

Another popular rider protects the contract owner's income. It allows the contract owner the peace of mind that if the market declines, their income base will not. This type of rider is a good option to consider if someone is planning their retirement and trying to insure income for their basic needs.

With riders and variable annuities there many different options and fees associated. It is important that you understand exactly how they work. Ask specific questions and get specific answers. Ask to see in writing the explanation the agent is giving. Most of the answers can be pointed out to you by the agent in the annuity prospectus or contract paperwork.

Which annuity is right for you?

The majority of your decisions will be based on how you want your money invested. If you need the largest possible income immediately, then you likely will want to consider an immediate annuity. As for deferred annuities, there are many options. Don't let that overwhelm you. Work with an advisor you trust and who will be patient to answer all of your questions.

The fact is that fixed rate, fixed index, and variable annuities are all very popular. The type that is best for you will depend on your time horizon, your other current investments, your goals and objectives, and your personal risk tolerance level.

As all investments do, annuities have pros and cons. One of the big complaints about annuities is that some have high fees and pay large commissions. This is true in some cases, but there are annuities that have extremely low costs, pay no commissions, and have no surrender charges. Take your time and clearly know why you are choosing any investment vehicle. I believe if they are used correctly and in the right circumstances, annuities can be very useful.

Chapter 5

Understanding Your Risk Tolerance

How do you view risk? Most likely your view has been partly determined by your personal experiences. If throughout your life you have not experienced great losses or major dishonesty, you may feel comfortable with some level of risk. On the other hand, if you have invested money and lost a good portion of it, or you have been taken advantage of by someone that used tricks, lies, or misleading information, you may be very cautious.

Regardless of your view of risk, it is very important that you completely understand how you personally feel about it. Why is that important? Think of it this way—have you ever ridden in a car that was being driven too fast?

Or one being driven too slow? Now imagine being stuck in that same car for hours on a long road trip. You would not want to be in either situation. Both extremes can be frustrating and give way to uncomfortable emotions. The longer we are in uncomfortable situations, the more our anxiety increases. It would be a much more enjoyable trip if you were in a car driven at the speed and level of safety that you most prefer.

The same is true when it comes to your retirement planning. It is like a long road trip and your comfort throughout the journey largely depends upon the amount of risk taken. For example, some individuals love the way the stock market works, while others may get physically sick at the thought of its volatility. Some may have a great pension that provides secured income regardless of how long they live and another may not have any secured income. Many factors affect how you feel about risk. The way you view risk will determine how you make decisions and which course you take on your retirement "road trip." In its most general terms, risk tolerance represents a tradeoff between fear and greed. As you make investment decisions and choices, you will find yourself in a balancing act between regret of losses incurred by taking too much risk and gains lost by taking too little.

How can risk tolerance be measured and how do you gauge your own personal comfort zone of risk? This is not an easy task. When it comes to a person's feelings, very little is cut and dried. You can't just ask someone, "How do you view risk?" Recent experiences can distort your perspective. Suppose you were in a bad car wreck last week. Because of that, your level of caution today likely would be much higher than normal. With time, however, you would gradually return to the way you normally drive. It would be nearly impossible to form an accurate picture of how you drive if someone asked you about your driving habits right after the wreck. The same is true in other areas of your life. More details and background are needed to form a more complete picture.

This leads us to an area of psychological testing known as psychometrics. Breaking down that word to its most basic parts, we get "psycho" meaning "of the mind" and "metric" meaning to measure. We can infer that this branch of psychology helps us measure the mind. Psychometric testing can be used to measure attitudes, personality traits, abilities, and knowledge. These measures are typically done using questionnaires or various kinds of tests or assessments. Some financial analysts may use a psychometric test to get an accurate reading of your risk tolerance.

As alluded to above, the questions on these types of test won't ask, "How do you view risk?" A good test will have gone through a rigorous development process. The questions likely will ask about your various preferences, values, or attitudes. They will address risk in general and will not be specific to investment risk or even financial risk in order not to provide skewed answers. A good test will have questions written in plain English and will avoid the use of financial terms that may be confusing. There should be a minimum of 20 questions so that results will be statistically relevant. The firm that developed the test should be able to provide sufficient evidence to support using the test as a standard.

What can a risk tolerance test reveal?

The answers you give to a risk tolerance test will help you understand your financial self better. If you are part of a couple and are investing together, both you and your partner should take the test. This will provide a clearer idea of you and your partner's attitudes about financial risk. It is likely that you and your spouse have different levels of risk tolerance. This is true for most couples. You both could probably give an accurate account of who is the most risk tolerant. However, you may not be aware of how wide the disparity is or the reasons for the variation of opinion. Reviewing a detailed risk profile report can offer that big picture view of your differences.

Knowing how and why you and your partner differ will help you understand each other better. It will also help you make better joint financial decisions that you both are comfortable with. A good financial advisor will be able to offer several alternative strategies to help you negotiate your differences and come to amicable decisions that suit you both. When it comes to risk tolerance, a financial advisor cannot make decisions for you. But a good advisor should be able to help you make decisions that allow you both to stay within your financial and risk tolerance comfort zones.

Understand how your advisor assesses risk tolerance

We have already established that the level of risk you can stand affects how psychologically receptive you are to decisions involving risk. Your level of risk tolerance also determines the anxiety you feel in risky situations. As was mentioned earlier, risk tolerance represents a trade-off between fear and greed. To what extent are you prepared to risk a less favorable outcome by pursuing a more favorable outcome? "Nothing ventured, nothing gained" may be viewed as a cliché by many, but most of us recognize the universal truth in its meaning. How much will you risk in order to gain? You have to determine where you are psychologically comfortable setting the balance point between fear and greed. The area of this balance point could be described as your financial comfort zone. By taking too few risks, you may feel you are missing out on opportunities. If you take on too much risk, you may be plagued with anxiety and worry.

It is essential that your financial advisor gets as good an understanding as possible of your risk tolerance. Unfortunately, accurately assessing a client's risk tolerance is often a failing of financial advisors. The average financial advisor is significantly more risk tolerant than the average client. Your advisor should not be suggesting investments to you based on his or her risk tolerance.

When seeking a new advisor or talking with your current advisor, ask them to explain how they view your risk tolerance. Ask how they came to their conclusions. Did they use psychometric testing to help them define your risk aversion? If so, are those tests standardized and can the publisher of the test prove its scientific validity? When they suggest financial solutions, make sure they fall within your financial comfort zone. Your advisor should be able to provide alternatives that meet your personal level of tolerance.

Risk tolerances change over time

Your financial plan is not set-it-and-forget-it. You need to review your circumstances regularly. In the same way, your risk tolerance should be reviewed regularly. Life events can influence you. Any major event—good or bad—should trigger a risk tolerance review. Otherwise, a review every two or three years is appropriate.

Learn how you and your spouse view risk. Ask your advisor how he or she assesses risk aversion in their clients. Have a thorough understanding of your risk tolerance before and throughout your retirement. This knowledge will aid tremendously in having peace of mind about your retirement plan and investments.

Chapter 6
Know Your Advisor

The statement "know your advisor" may sound a little silly. You may ask yourself, "Who does not know their advisor?" How could someone hire an advisor and not know them? You may know their name, where their office is located, and may even know their family. I feel you should know more than just the basics about your financial advisor. For instance, do you know exactly how your advisor gets paid and what their responsibility is to you? Is your advisor held to a fiduciary standard? Do they have a system in place to communicate with you regularly? Do you have a written document called an Investment Policy Statement? These are just a few questions we will consider in this chapter.

Commissions and fees

Individuals come into my office all the time and tell me they have been with a certain advisor for a few years. They state that they like and trust them. I then ask how their advisor gets paid. Most do not know. They assume their advisor gets paid by the mutual fund or the annuity company. Some say they pay their advisor a fee and others say their advisors receive some combination of commission and fees. When I ask what is the fee, most do not know! You should ask and know the answer to the question, "How does my advisor get paid?"

Understanding exactly how your advisor is compensated is very important. Consider this: If your advisor only receives a commission when they sell you something or change your mutual funds, how much can you trust their recommendations? If they are paid by fee only, that makes it important to understand what the fee is and how they charge it.

If you are interviewing a new advisor, make sure you ask about their compensation up front. If the advisor is trying to sell you a product that is on a commission basis, you should know. By no means am I saying that commissions are wrong. What I am saying is that you should understand how your advisor gets paid. If you know how they are getting paid you can then ask why a particular product or service is being recommended. You could also ask if the advisor shopped around for the best, lowest cost product or if they chose a product that pays the highest commission.

Knowing how your advisor gets paid will help you tremendously. If your current advisor or an advisor you are considering hiring does not want to clearly answer questions about their compensation, that could be a sign they are trying to hide something. It may be an indication that they are not thinking of your best interest, but possibly of their own best interest. I encourage you to consider a different advisor if this is the case.

Is your advisor held to a fiduciary standard?

In the financial services industry, there are brokers and there are advisors. There are people who sell products and people who sell knowledge. There are people who look out for their commissions and people who look out for you. The difference is a fiduciary standard. Merriam-Webster's defines fiduciary as "held or founded in trust or confidence." A fiduciary standard is about your interests, goals, and well-being. Do you know if your financial advisor is held to a fiduciary standard? I think they should be, to protect you and your financial livelihood. Do you expect your doctor or lawyer to put your interests first? Of course you do; doctors and lawyers are held to a fiduciary standard. As for financial advisors, the fact is many are not held to this high standard. Do you want your advisor to be required to put your interests first? If you currently have an advisor, ask them if they are required by law to put your interests first. If you are interviewing an advisor, make sure they are held to a fiduciary standard before you do business with them.

A Registered Investment Advisor (RIA) is a person or company that has registered with the U.S. Securities and Exchange Commission (SEC) or with a State Securities Division. This registration does not mean the SEC approves, sanctions, or attests to the merits of the person or company. It simply indicates the person or entity is registered and has agreed to abide by certain fiduciary standards. An RIA may be registered with a State Securities Division as well as with the SEC. The RIA and Investment Advisor (IA) designations came about from the Investment Advisors Act of 1940. The fiduciary standard is based on the laws that this act put in place. The fiduciary standard means that an advisor is required to act only in the best interest of his or her client. This is true even if the interest conflicts with the advisor's financial interests. An advisor held to this standard is required to report any conflicts or potential conflicts of interest before and during the time the advisor is engaged by the client. Additionally, RIAs and IAs must disclose how they are compensated and agree to abide by a code of ethics. Very few who claim to be financial advisors are actually federally- or state-registered. Most are considered to be broker-dealers, which are held to lower and non-regulated standards. Federal law requires broker-dealers to act in the best interest of their employer—not their clients. This does not mean they are unethical or plan to harm their clients. In fact, I feel confident most are ethical and do not intend harm to their clients. The scary thing is that they are not required by law to act in their client's best interest. If your advisor is not required to act in your best interest, then this limits your recourse if you feel you have been taken advantage of.

To guard against unethical violations, the SEC requires broker-dealers to include the following disclosure in their client agreements. Read this disclosure. Is this the type of relationship you want with your advisor?

"Your account is a brokerage account and not an advisory account. Our interests may not always be the same as yours. Please ask us questions to make sure you understand your rights and our obligations to you, including the extent of our obligations to disclose conflicts of interest and to act in your best interest. We are paid both by you and, sometimes, by people who compensate us based on what you buy. Therefore, our profits, and our salespersons' compensation, may vary by product and over time."

If you have signed an agreement with an advisor, go look at it. Is this disclaimer in there? If so, ask your advisor for more details. Decide if the relationship is in your best interest.

What is an Investment Policy Statement?

Do you have an Investment Policy Statement (IPS)? What is it? An IPS is a written statement that details the policies, procedures, and goals that you and your advisor have agreed to in regards to managing your investments. This type of document is required when a fiduciary relationship exists. An IPS outlines a systematic approach for making decisions. It establishes a way to tackle difficult issues related to your investment choices. Having a plan provides clarity as you work with your advisor to meet certain expectations and goals. A well-thought-out statement helps your advisor understand what you expect. It also demonstrates your advisor's willingness to meet your investment needs and help you meet your goals.

What should an IPS include? It is advisable to include the following sections in the IPS:

- Objectives. In clearly defined language, the IPS should describe expectations, risk tolerance, return decisions, and guidelines for investments.

- Asset allocation policy. This section will categorize the asset classes you want in your portfolio and define how those assets are best allocated to meet your goals.

- Management procedures. This should outline how you want your investments monitored and evaluated. It should detail how and when changes should be managed.

- Communication procedures. Good communication is essential when it comes to your investments. This section should detail communication processes and objectives for the client and advisor. It should also assign responsibility for implementation.

Here are the steps needed to establish an investment policy:

1. Identify what your financial goals and needs are so you can determine your financial situation.

2. Establish your risk tolerance and your investment time horizon.

3. Set long term investment goals.

4. Decide what restrictions you have for your portfolio and assets.

5. Determine the asset classes and allocation that will maximize the likelihood of achieving your investment objectives at the lowest level of risk.

6. Decide how you want to handle investment selection, rebalancing, buy-sell principles, portfolio reviews, reporting, and so on.

7. Implement the decisions and review as necessary.

Lack of information and forethought causes investors to make inappropriate decisions. Emotions also factor in to poor decision-making. An IPS will provide investors with a written statement that can guide them to make prudent and rational decisions.

Certified Financial Planner™ Practitioner

Should your advisor be a Certified Financial Planner™ Practitioner?

Most likely the only one who would say no to this is an advisor who has not achieved the designation. Why should your advisor be one? When people hear the term "financial planner," they believe that person to have some sort of certification or to have undergone some level of training. In fact, that is not the case. Nearly anyone can get away with calling themselves a financial planner. However, it is only those who have fulfilled the requirements of the Certified Financial Planner Board of Standards who may use the CFP® certification mark. This mark can provide you with a sense of security in knowing that the person has met a baseline of training preparation. The requirements, outlined in detail below, are a combination of education, exams, years of experience, and adherence to an ethical code.

- Education. A CFP® practitioner must have a bachelor's degree from an accredited U.S. college or university, or an equivalent foreign university. Their studies must have included financial planning subject areas outlined by the CFP Board as necessary to become a competent financial planner. The subject areas encompass investment planning, income tax planning, insurance planning, employee benefits planning, risk management, as well as retirement and estate planning.

- Examination. To earn the CFP® certification, the person must pass a comprehensive 10-hour exam (taken over two days). The exam includes scenarios and case studies that determine one's ability to diagnose issues related to financial planning and apply their learned knowledge to real-world circumstances.

- Experience. To become a CFP® practitioner, the person must have a minimum of three years of full-time financial planning experience. This must equate to 2,000 hours per year.

- Ethics. The CFP Board has developed documents that detail the ethical and practice standards to be followed by CFP® professionals. Those with the CFP® designation agree to follow the Board's Standards of Professional Conduct.

After becoming certified, their training is not over. To continue using the CFP® designation, individuals must complete ongoing education and ethics training. This includes 30 hours of continuing education every two years. Two of those hours must be on the Code of Ethics and other parts of Standards of Professional Conduct. This training is intended to ensure that these professionals stay abreast of developments in the financial planning field. Furthermore, CFP® professionals have to renew their agreement to abide by the Standards of Professional Conduct. A major aspect of this agreement requires that CFP® professionals provide financial planning services at a fiduciary standard of care. They must offer financial planning services that align with the best interests of their clients.

CFP® professionals who fail to meet these requirements can be suspended or have their certification permanently revoked. When choosing a financial advisor, I recommend you consider working with a Certified Financial Planner™ Practitioner to provide you with added confidence in their abilities.

Act in your own best interest

There are other things to consider when choosing an advisor, but looking at the topics detailed in this chapter can be a great start. Choosing a competent financial advisor whom you trust may be one of the most important decisions you make. Not only can your choice impact you, it can also impact your loved ones. Choose your advisor wisely. The right advisor can be a guide to you and your family throughout your life as you address specific financial concerns. They can help you find financial peace of mind and assist you in achieving your life goals. Never let an advisor scare you into becoming a client or make you feel guilty in order to keep you as a client. Take the time to get complete answers to all of your questions. Above all, act in your own best interest.

Appendix A

IRS Publication 590 Table II —Joint Life and Last Survivor Expectancy

Ages	20	21	22	23	24	25	26	27	28	29
IRS Publication 590 Table II										
(Joint Life and Last Survivor Expectancy)										
(For Use by Owners Whose Spouses Are More Than 10 Years Younger and Are the Sole Beneficiaries of Their IRAs)										
20	70.1	69.6	69.1	68.7	68.3	67.9	67.5	67.2	66.9	66.6
21	69.6	69.1	68.6	68.2	67.7	67.3	66.9	66.6	66.2	65.9
22	69.1	68.6	68.1	67.6	67.2	66.7	66.3	65.9	65.6	65.2
23	68.7	68.2	67.6	67.1	66.6	66.2	65.7	65.3	64.9	64.6
24	68.3	67.7	67.2	66.6	66.1	65.6	65.2	64.7	64.3	63.9
25	67.9	67.3	66.7	66.2	65.6	65.1	64.6	64.2	63.7	63.3
26	67.5	66.9	66.3	65.7	65.2	64.6	64.1	63.6	63.2	62.8
27	67.2	66.6	65.9	65.3	64.7	64.2	63.6	63.1	62.7	62.2
28	66.9	66.2	65.6	64.9	64.3	63.7	63.2	62.7	62.1	61.7
29	66.6	65.9	65.2	64.6	63.9	63.3	62.8	62.2	61.7	61.2
30	66.3	65.6	64.9	64.2	63.6	62.9	62.3	61.8	61.2	60.7
31	66.1	65.3	64.6	63.9	63.2	62.6	62.0	61.4	60.8	60.2
32	65.8	65.1	64.3	63.6	62.9	62.2	61.6	61.0	60.4	59.8
33	65.6	64.8	64.1	63.3	62.6	61.9	61.3	60.6	60.0	59.4
34	65.4	64.6	63.8	63.1	62.3	61.6	60.9	60.3	59.6	59.0
35	65.2	64.4	63.6	62.8	62.1	61.4	60.6	59.9	59.3	58.6
36	65.0	64.2	63.4	62.6	61.9	61.1	60.4	59.6	59.0	58.3
37	64.9	64.0	63.2	62.4	61.6	60.9	60.1	59.4	58.7	58.0
38	64.7	63.9	63.0	62.2	61.4	60.6	59.9	59.1	58.4	57.7
39	64.6	63.7	62.9	62.1	61.2	60.4	59.6	58.9	58.1	57.4
40	64.4	63.6	62.7	61.9	61.1	60.2	59.4	58.7	57.9	57.1
41	64.3	63.5	62.6	61.7	60.9	60.1	59.3	58.5	57.7	56.9
42	64.2	63.3	62.5	61.6	60.8	59.9	59.1	58.3	57.5	56.7
43	64.1	63.2	62.4	61.5	60.6	59.8	58.9	58.1	57.3	56.5
44	64.0	63.1	62.2	61.4	60.5	59.6	58.8	57.9	57.1	56.3
45	64.0	63.0	62.2	61.3	60.4	59.5	58.6	57.8	56.9	56.1

Ages	20	21	22	23	24	25	26	27	28	29
	IRS Publication 590 Table II (continued)									
	(Joint Life and Last Survivor Expectancy)									
	(For Use by Owners Whose Spouses Are More Than 10 Years									
	Younger and Are the Sole Beneficiaries of Their IRAs)									
46	63.9	63.0	62.1	61.2	60.3	59.4	58.5	57.7	56.8	56.0
47	63.8	62.9	62.0	61.1	60.2	59.3	58.4	57.5	56.7	55.8
48	63.7	62.8	61.9	61.0	60.1	59.2	58.3	57.4	56.5	55.7
49	63.7	62.8	61.8	60.9	60.0	59.1	58.2	57.3	56.4	55.6
50	63.6	62.7	61.8	60.8	59.9	59.0	58.1	57.2	56.3	55.4
51	63.6	62.6	61.7	60.8	59.9	58.9	58.0	57.1	56.2	55.3
52	63.5	62.6	61.7	60.7	59.8	58.9	58.0	57.1	56.1	55.2
53	63.5	62.5	61.6	60.7	59.7	58.8	57.9	57.0	56.1	55.2
54	63.5	62.5	61.6	60.6	59.7	58.8	57.8	56.9	56.0	55.1
55	63.4	62.5	61.5	60.6	59.6	58.7	57.8	56.8	55.9	55.0
56	63.4	62.4	61.5	60.5	59.6	58.7	57.7	56.8	55.9	54.9
57	63.4	62.4	61.5	60.5	59.6	58.6	57.7	56.7	55.8	54.9
58	63.3	62.4	61.4	60.5	59.5	58.6	57.6	56.7	55.8	54.8
59	63.3	62.3	61.4	60.4	59.5	58.5	57.6	56.7	55.7	54.8
60	63.3	62.3	61.4	60.4	59.5	58.5	57.6	56.6	55.7	54.7
61	63.3	62.3	61.3	60.4	59.4	58.5	57.5	56.6	55.6	54.7
62	63.2	62.3	61.3	60.4	59.4	58.4	57.5	56.5	55.6	54.7
63	63.2	62.3	61.3	60.3	59.4	58.4	57.5	56.5	55.6	54.6
64	63.2	62.2	61.3	60.3	59.4	58.4	57.4	56.5	55.5	54.6
65	63.2	62.2	61.3	60.3	59.3	58.4	57.4	56.5	55.5	54.6
66	63.2	62.2	61.2	60.3	59.3	58.4	57.4	56.4	55.5	54.5
67	63.2	62.2	61.2	60.3	59.3	58.3	57.4	56.4	55.5	54.5
68	63.1	62.2	61.2	60.2	59.3	58.3	57.4	56.4	55.4	54.5
69	63.1	62.2	61.2	60.2	59.3	58.3	57.3	56.4	55.4	54.5
70	63.1	62.2	61.2	60.2	59.3	58.3	57.3	56.4	55.4	54.4
71	63.1	62.1	61.2	60.2	59.2	58.3	57.3	56.4	55.4	54.4

IRS Publication 590 Table II (continued) (Joint Life and Last Survivor Expectancy) (For Use by Owners Whose Spouses Are More Than 10 Years Younger and Are the Sole Beneficiaries of Their IRAs)									
Ages	20	21	22	23	24	25	26	27	28	29
72	63.1	62.1	61.2	60.2	59.2	58.3	57.3	56.3	55.4	54.4
73	63.1	62.1	61.2	60.2	59.2	58.3	57.3	56.3	55.4	54.4
74	63.1	62.1	61.2	60.2	59.2	58.2	57.3	56.3	55.4	54.4
75	63.1	62.1	61.1	60.2	59.2	58.2	57.3	56.3	55.3	54.4
76	63.1	62.1	61.1	60.2	59.2	58.2	57.3	56.3	55.3	54.4
77	63.1	62.1	61.1	60.2	59.2	58.2	57.3	56.3	55.3	54.4
78	63.1	62.1	61.1	60.2	59.2	58.2	57.3	56.3	55.3	54.4
79	63.1	62.1	61.1	60.2	59.2	58.2	57.2	56.3	55.3	54.3
80	63.1	62.1	61.1	60.1	59.2	58.2	57.2	56.3	55.3	54.3
81	63.1	62.1	61.1	60.1	59.2	58.2	57.2	56.3	55.3	54.3
82	63.1	62.1	61.1	60.1	59.2	58.2	57.2	56.3	55.3	54.3
83	63.1	62.1	61.1	60.1	59.2	58.2	57.2	56.3	55.3	54.3
84	63.0	62.1	61.1	60.1	59.2	58.2	57.2	56.3	55.3	54.3
85	63.0	62.1	61.1	60.1	59.2	58.2	57.2	56.3	55.3	54.3
86	63.0	62.1	61.1	60.1	59.2	58.2	57.2	56.2	55.3	54.3
87	63.0	62.1	61.1	60.1	59.2	58.2	57.2	56.2	55.3	54.3
88	63.0	62.1	61.1	60.1	59.2	58.2	57.2	56.2	55.3	54.3
89	63.0	62.1	61.1	60.1	59.1	58.2	57.2	56.2	55.3	54.3
90	63.0	62.1	61.1	60.1	59.1	58.2	57.2	56.2	55.3	54.3
91	63.0	62.1	61.1	60.1	59.1	58.2	57.2	56.2	55.3	54.3
92	63.0	62.1	61.1	60.1	59.1	58.2	57.2	56.2	55.3	54.3
93	63.0	62.1	61.1	60.1	59.1	58.2	57.2	56.2	55.3	54.3
94	63.0	62.1	61.1	60.1	59.1	58.2	57.2	56.2	55.3	54.3
95	63.0	62.1	61.1	60.1	59.1	58.2	57.2	56.2	55.3	54.3
96	63.0	62.1	61.1	60.1	59.1	58.2	57.2	56.2	55.3	54.3
97	63.0	62.1	61.1	60.1	59.1	58.2	57.2	56.2	55.3	54.3

IRS Publication 590 Table II (continued) (Joint Life and Last Survivor Expectancy) (For Use by Owners Whose Spouses Are More Than 10 Years Younger and Are the Sole Beneficiaries of Their IRAs)									
Ages	**20**	**21**	**22**	**23**	**24**	**25**	**26**	**27**	**28**	**29**
98	63.0	62.1	61.1	60.1	59.1	58.2	57.2	56.2	55.3	54.3
99	63.0	62.1	61.1	60.1	59.1	58.2	57.2	56.2	55.3	54.3
100	63.0	62.1	61.1	60.1	59.1	58.2	57.2	56.2	55.3	54.3
101	63.0	62.1	61.1	60.1	59.1	58.2	57.2	56.2	55.3	54.3
102	63.0	62.1	61.1	60.1	59.1	58.2	57.2	56.2	55.3	54.3
103	63.0	62.1	61.1	60.1	59.1	58.2	57.2	56.2	55.3	54.3
104	63.0	62.1	61.1	60.1	59.1	58.2	57.2	56.2	55.3	54.3
105	63.0	62.1	61.1	60.1	59.1	58.2	57.2	56.2	55.3	54.3
106	63.0	62.1	61.1	60.1	59.1	58.2	57.2	56.2	55.3	54.3
107	63.0	62.1	61.1	60.1	59.1	58.2	57.2	56.2	55.3	54.3
108	63.0	62.1	61.1	60.1	59.1	58.2	57.2	56.2	55.3	54.3
109	63.0	62.1	61.1	60.1	59.1	58.2	57.2	56.2	55.3	54.3
110	63.0	62.1	61.1	60.1	59.1	58.2	57.2	56.2	55.3	54.3
111	63.0	62.1	61.1	60.1	59.1	58.2	57.2	56.2	55.3	54.3
112	63.0	62.1	61.1	60.1	59.1	58.2	57.2	56.2	55.3	54.3
113	63.0	62.1	61.1	60.1	59.1	58.2	57.2	56.2	55.3	54.3
114	63.0	62.1	61.1	60.1	59.1	58.2	57.2	56.2	55.3	54.3
115+	63.0	62.1	61.1	60.1	59.1	58.2	57.2	56.2	55.3	54.3
Ages	**30**	**31**	**32**	**33**	**34**	**35**	**36**	**37**	**38**	**39**
30	60.2	59.7	59.2	58.8	58.4	58.0	57.6	57.3	57.0	56.7
31	59.7	59.2	58.7	58.2	57.8	57.4	57.0	56.6	56.3	56.0
32	59.2	58.7	58.2	57.7	57.2	56.8	56.4	56.0	55.6	55.3
33	58.8	58.2	57.7	57.2	56.7	56.2	55.8	55.4	55.0	54.7
34	58.4	57.8	57.2	56.7	56.2	55.7	55.3	54.8	54.4	54.0
35	58.0	57.4	56.8	56.2	55.7	55.2	54.7	54.3	53.8	53.4
36	57.6	57.0	56.4	55.8	55.3	54.7	54.2	53.7	53.3	52.8

Ages	30	31	32	33	34	35	36	37	38	39
	IRS Publication 590 Table II (continued) (Joint Life and Last Survivor Expectancy) (For Use by Owners Whose Spouses Are More Than 10 Years Younger and Are the Sole Beneficiaries of Their IRAs)									
37	57.3	56.6	56.0	55.4	54.8	54.3	53.7	53.2	52.7	52.3
38	57.0	56.3	55.6	55.0	54.4	53.8	53.3	52.7	52.2	51.7
39	56.7	56.0	55.3	54.7	54.0	53.4	52.8	52.3	51.7	51.2
40	56.4	55.7	55.0	54.3	53.7	53.0	52.4	51.8	51.3	50.8
41	56.1	55.4	54.7	54.0	53.3	52.7	52.0	51.4	50.9	50.3
42	55.9	55.2	54.4	53.7	53.0	52.3	51.7	51.1	50.4	49.9
43	55.7	54.9	54.2	53.4	52.7	52.0	51.3	50.7	50.1	49.5
44	55.5	54.7	53.9	53.2	52.4	51.7	51.0	50.4	49.7	49.1
45	55.3	54.5	53.7	52.9	52.2	51.5	50.7	50.0	49.4	48.7
46	55.1	54.3	53.5	52.7	52.0	51.2	50.5	49.8	49.1	48.4
47	55.0	54.1	53.3	52.5	51.7	51.0	50.2	49.5	48.8	48.1
48	54.8	54.0	53.2	52.3	51.5	50.8	50.0	49.2	48.5	47.8
49	54.7	53.8	53.0	52.2	51.4	50.6	49.8	49.0	48.2	47.5
50	54.6	53.7	52.9	52.0	51.2	50.4	49.6	48.8	48.0	47.3
51	54.5	53.6	52.7	51.9	51.0	50.2	49.4	48.6	47.8	47.0
52	54.4	53.5	52.6	51.7	50.9	50.0	49.2	48.4	47.6	46.8
53	54.3	53.4	52.5	51.6	50.8	49.9	49.1	48.2	47.4	46.6
54	54.2	53.3	52.4	51.5	50.6	49.8	48.9	48.1	47.2	46.4
55	54.1	53.2	52.3	51.4	50.5	49.7	48.8	47.9	47.1	46.3
56	54.0	53.1	52.2	51.3	50.4	49.5	48.7	47.8	47.0	46.1
57	54.0	53.0	52.1	51.2	50.3	49.4	48.6	47.7	46.8	46.0
58	53.9	53.0	52.1	51.2	50.3	49.4	48.5	47.6	46.7	45.8
59	53.8	52.9	52.0	51.1	50.2	49.3	48.4	47.5	46.6	45.7
60	53.8	52.9	51.9	51.0	50.1	49.2	48.3	47.4	46.5	45.6
61	53.8	52.8	51.9	51.0	50.0	49.1	48.2	47.3	46.4	45.5
62	53.7	52.8	51.8	50.9	50.0	49.1	48.1	47.2	46.3	45.4

IRS Publication 590 Table II (continued) (Joint Life and Last Survivor Expectancy) (For Use by Owners Whose Spouses Are More Than 10 Years Younger and Are the Sole Beneficiaries of Their IRAs)									
Ages	30	31	32	33	34	35	36	37	38	39
63	53.7	52.7	51.8	50.9	49.9	49.0	48.1	47.2	46.3	45.3
64	53.6	52.7	51.8	50.8	49.9	48.9	48.0	47.1	46.2	45.3
65	53.6	52.7	51.7	50.8	49.8	48.9	48.0	47.0	46.1	45.2
66	53.6	52.6	51.7	50.7	49.8	48.9	47.9	47.0	46.1	45.1
67	53.6	52.6	51.7	50.7	49.8	48.8	47.9	46.9	46.0	45.1
68	53.5	52.6	51.6	50.7	49.7	48.8	47.8	46.9	46.0	45.0
69	53.5	52.6	51.6	50.6	49.7	48.7	47.8	46.9	45.9	45.0
70	53.5	52.5	51.6	50.6	49.7	48.7	47.8	46.8	45.9	44.9
71	53.5	52.5	51.6	50.6	49.6	48.7	47.7	46.8	45.9	44.9
72	53.5	52.5	51.5	50.6	49.6	48.7	47.7	46.8	45.8	44.9
73	53.4	52.5	51.5	50.6	49.6	48.6	47.7	46.7	45.8	44.8
74	53.4	52.5	51.5	50.5	49.6	48.6	47.7	46.7	45.8	44.8
75	53.4	52.5	51.5	50.5	49.6	48.6	47.7	46.7	45.7	44.8
76	53.4	52.4	51.5	50.5	49.6	48.6	47.6	46.7	45.7	44.8
77	53.4	52.4	51.5	50.5	49.5	48.6	47.6	46.7	45.7	44.8
78	53.4	52.4	51.5	50.5	49.5	48.6	47.6	46.6	45.7	44.7
79	53.4	52.4	51.5	50.5	49.5	48.6	47.6	46.6	45.7	44.7
80	53.4	52.4	51.4	50.5	49.5	48.5	47.6	46.6	45.7	44.7
81	53.4	52.4	51.4	50.5	49.5	48.5	47.6	46.6	45.7	44.7
82	53.4	52.4	51.4	50.5	49.5	48.5	47.6	46.6	45.6	44.7
83	53.4	52.4	51.4	50.5	49.5	48.5	47.6	46.6	45.6	44.7
84	53.4	52.4	51.4	50.5	49.5	48.5	47.6	46.6	45.6	44.7
85	53.3	52.4	51.4	50.4	49.5	48.5	47.5	46.6	45.6	44.7
86	53.3	52.4	51.4	50.4	49.5	48.5	47.5	46.6	45.6	44.6
87	53.3	52.4	51.4	50.4	49.5	48.5	47.5	46.6	45.6	44.6
88	53.3	52.4	51.4	50.4	49.5	48.5	47.5	46.6	45.6	44.6

Ages	30	31	32	33	34	35	36	37	38	39

IRS Publication 590 Table II (continued)
(Joint Life and Last Survivor Expectancy)
(For Use by Owners Whose Spouses Are More Than 10 Years Younger and Are the Sole Beneficiaries of Their IRAs)

Ages	30	31	32	33	34	35	36	37	38	39
89	53.3	52.4	51.4	50.4	49.5	48.5	47.5	46.6	45.6	44.6
90	53.3	52.4	51.4	50.4	49.5	48.5	47.5	46.6	45.6	44.6
91	53.3	52.4	51.4	50.4	49.5	48.5	47.5	46.6	45.6	44.6
92	53.3	52.4	51.4	50.4	49.5	48.5	47.5	46.6	45.6	44.6
93	53.3	52.4	51.4	50.4	49.5	48.5	47.5	46.6	45.6	44.6
94	53.3	52.4	51.4	50.4	49.5	48.5	47.5	46.6	45.6	44.6
95	53.3	52.4	51.4	50.4	49.5	48.5	47.5	46.5	45.6	44.6
96	53.3	52.4	51.4	50.4	49.5	48.5	47.5	46.5	45.6	44.6
97	53.3	52.4	51.4	50.4	49.5	48.5	47.5	46.5	45.6	44.6
98	53.3	52.4	51.4	50.4	49.5	48.5	47.5	46.5	45.6	44.6
99	53.3	52.4	51.4	50.4	49.5	48.5	47.5	46.5	45.6	44.6
100	53.3	52.4	51.4	50.4	49.5	48.5	47.5	46.5	45.6	44.6
101	53.3	52.4	51.4	50.4	49.5	48.5	47.5	46.5	45.6	44.6
102	53.3	52.4	51.4	50.4	49.5	48.5	47.5	46.5	45.6	44.6
103	53.3	52.4	51.4	50.4	49.5	48.5	47.5	46.5	45.6	44.6
104	53.3	52.4	51.4	50.4	49.5	48.5	47.5	46.5	45.6	44.6
105	53.3	52.4	51.4	50.4	49.4	48.5	47.5	46.5	45.6	44.6
106	53.3	52.4	51.4	50.4	49.4	48.5	47.5	46.5	45.6	44.6
107	53.3	52.4	51.4	50.4	49.4	48.5	47.5	46.5	45.6	44.6
108	53.3	52.4	51.4	50.4	49.4	48.5	47.5	46.5	45.6	44.6
109	53.3	52.4	51.4	50.4	49.4	48.5	47.5	46.5	45.6	44.6
110	53.3	52.4	51.4	50.4	49.4	48.5	47.5	46.5	45.6	44.6
111	53.3	52.4	51.4	50.4	49.4	48.5	47.5	46.5	45.6	44.6
112	53.3	52.4	51.4	50.4	49.4	48.5	47.5	46.5	45.6	44.6
113	53.3	52.4	51.4	50.4	49.4	48.5	47.5	46.5	45.6	44.6
114	53.3	52.4	51.4	50.4	49.4	48.5	47.5	46.5	45.6	44.6

IRS Publication 590 Table II (continued) (Joint Life and Last Survivor Expectancy) (For Use by Owners Whose Spouses Are More Than 10 Years Younger and Are the Sole Beneficiaries of Their IRAs)									
Ages	30	31	32	33	34	35	36	37	38	39
115+	53.3	52.4	51.4	50.4	49.4	48.5	47.5	46.5	45.6	44.6
Ages	40	41	42	43	44	45	46	47	48	49
40	50.2	49.8	49.3	48.9	48.5	48.1	47.7	47.4	47.1	46.8
41	49.8	49.3	48.8	48.3	47.9	47.5	47.1	46.7	46.4	46.1
42	49.3	48.8	48.3	47.8	47.3	46.9	46.5	46.1	45.8	45.4
43	48.9	48.3	47.8	47.3	46.8	46.3	45.9	45.5	45.1	44.8
44	48.5	47.9	47.3	46.8	46.3	45.8	45.4	44.9	44.5	44.2
45	48.1	47.5	46.9	46.3	45.8	45.3	44.8	44.4	44.0	43.6
46	47.7	47.1	46.5	45.9	45.4	44.8	44.3	43.9	43.4	43.0
47	47.4	46.7	46.1	45.5	44.9	44.4	43.9	43.4	42.9	42.4
48	47.1	46.4	45.8	45.1	44.5	44.0	43.4	42.9	42.4	41.9
49	46.8	46.1	45.4	44.8	44.2	43.6	43.0	42.4	41.9	41.4
50	46.5	45.8	45.1	44.4	43.8	43.2	42.6	42.0	41.5	40.9
51	46.3	45.5	44.8	44.1	43.5	42.8	42.2	41.6	41.0	40.5
52	46.0	45.3	44.6	43.8	43.2	42.5	41.8	41.2	40.6	40.1
53	45.8	45.1	44.3	43.6	42.9	42.2	41.5	40.9	40.3	39.7
54	45.6	44.8	44.1	43.3	42.6	41.9	41.2	40.5	39.9	39.3
55	45.5	44.7	43.9	43.1	42.4	41.6	40.9	40.2	39.6	38.9
56	45.3	44.5	43.7	42.9	42.1	41.4	40.7	40.0	39.3	38.6
57	45.1	44.3	43.5	42.7	41.9	41.2	40.4	39.7	39.0	38.3
58	45.0	44.2	43.3	42.5	41.7	40.9	40.2	39.4	38.7	38.0
59	44.9	44.0	43.2	42.4	41.5	40.7	40.0	39.2	38.5	37.8
60	44.7	43.9	43.0	42.2	41.4	40.6	39.8	39.0	38.2	37.5
61	44.6	43.8	42.9	42.1	41.2	40.4	39.6	38.8	38.0	37.3
62	44.5	43.7	42.8	41.9	41.1	40.3	39.4	38.6	37.8	37.1
63	44.5	43.6	42.7	41.8	41.0	40.1	39.3	38.5	37.7	36.9

Ages	40	41	42	43	44	45	46	47	48	49
64	44.4	43.5	42.6	41.7	40.8	40.0	39.2	38.3	37.5	36.7
65	44.3	43.4	42.5	41.6	40.7	39.9	39.0	38.2	37.4	36.6
66	44.2	43.3	42.4	41.5	40.6	39.8	38.9	38.1	37.2	36.4
67	44.2	43.3	42.3	41.4	40.6	39.7	38.8	38.0	37.1	36.3
68	44.1	43.2	42.3	41.4	40.5	39.6	38.7	37.9	37.0	36.2
69	44.1	43.1	42.2	41.3	40.4	39.5	38.6	37.8	36.9	36.0
70	44.0	43.1	42.2	41.3	40.3	39.4	38.6	37.7	36.8	35.9
71	44.0	43.0	42.1	41.2	40.3	39.4	38.5	37.6	36.7	35.9
72	43.9	43.0	42.1	41.1	40.2	39.3	38.4	37.5	36.6	35.8
73	43.9	43.0	42.0	41.1	40.2	39.3	38.4	37.5	36.6	35.7
74	43.9	42.9	42.0	41.1	40.1	39.2	38.3	37.4	36.5	35.6
75	43.8	42.9	42.0	41.0	40.1	39.2	38.3	37.4	36.5	35.6
76	43.8	42.9	41.9	41.0	40.1	39.1	38.2	37.3	36.4	35.5
77	43.8	42.9	41.9	41.0	40.0	39.1	38.2	37.3	36.4	35.5
78	43.8	42.8	41.9	40.9	40.0	39.1	38.2	37.2	36.3	35.4
79	43.8	42.8	41.9	40.9	40.0	39.1	38.1	37.2	36.3	35.4
80	43.7	42.8	41.8	40.9	40.0	39.0	38.1	37.2	36.3	35.4
81	43.7	42.8	41.8	40.9	39.9	39.0	38.1	37.2	36.2	35.3
82	43.7	42.8	41.8	40.9	39.9	39.0	38.1	37.1	36.2	35.3
83	43.7	42.8	41.8	40.9	39.9	39.0	38.0	37.1	36.2	35.3
84	43.7	42.7	41.8	40.8	39.9	39.0	38.0	37.1	36.2	35.3
85	43.7	42.7	41.8	40.8	39.9	38.9	38.0	37.1	36.2	35.2
86	43.7	42.7	41.8	40.8	39.9	38.9	38.0	37.1	36.1	35.2
87	43.7	42.7	41.8	40.8	39.9	38.9	38.0	37.0	36.1	35.2
88	43.7	42.7	41.8	40.8	39.9	38.9	38.0	37.0	36.1	35.2
89	43.7	42.7	41.7	40.8	39.8	38.9	38.0	37.0	36.1	35.2

IRS Publication 590 Table II (continued)
(Joint Life and Last Survivor Expectancy)
(For Use by Owners Whose Spouses Are More Than 10 Years Younger and Are the Sole Beneficiaries of Their IRAs)

Ages	40	41	42	43	44	45	46	47	48	49
IRS Publication 590 Table II (continued)										
(Joint Life and Last Survivor Expectancy)										
(For Use by Owners Whose Spouses Are More Than 10 Years										
Younger and Are the Sole Beneficiaries of Their IRAs)										
90	43.7	42.7	41.7	40.8	39.8	38.9	38.0	37.0	36.1	35.2
91	43.7	42.7	41.7	40.8	39.8	38.9	37.9	37.0	36.1	35.2
92	43.7	42.7	41.7	40.8	39.8	38.9	37.9	37.0	36.1	35.1
93	43.7	42.7	41.7	40.8	39.8	38.9	37.9	37.0	36.1	35.1
94	43.7	42.7	41.7	40.8	39.8	38.9	37.9	37.0	36.1	35.1
95	43.6	42.7	41.7	40.8	39.8	38.9	37.9	37.0	36.1	35.1
96	43.6	42.7	41.7	40.8	39.8	38.9	37.9	37.0	36.1	35.1
97	43.6	42.7	41.7	40.8	39.8	38.9	37.9	37.0	36.1	35.1
98	43.6	42.7	41.7	40.8	39.8	38.9	37.9	37.0	36.0	35.1
99	43.6	42.7	41.7	40.8	39.8	38.9	37.9	37.0	36.0	35.1
100	43.6	42.7	41.7	40.8	39.8	38.9	37.9	37.0	36.0	35.1
101	43.6	42.7	41.7	40.8	39.8	38.9	37.9	37.0	36.0	35.1
102	43.6	42.7	41.7	40.8	39.8	38.9	37.9	37.0	36.0	35.1
103	43.6	42.7	41.7	40.8	39.8	38.9	37.9	37.0	36.0	35.1
104	43.6	42.7	41.7	40.8	39.8	38.8	37.9	37.0	36.0	35.1
105	43.6	42.7	41.7	40.8	39.8	38.8	37.9	37.0	36.0	35.1
106	43.6	42.7	41.7	40.8	39.8	38.8	37.9	37.0	36.0	35.1
107	43.6	42.7	41.7	40.8	39.8	38.8	37.9	37.0	36.0	35.1
108	43.6	42.7	41.7	40.8	39.8	38.8	37.9	37.0	36.0	35.1
109	43.6	42.7	41.7	40.7	39.8	38.8	37.9	37.0	36.0	35.1
110	43.6	42.7	41.7	40.7	39.8	38.8	37.9	37.0	36.0	35.1
111	43.6	42.7	41.7	40.7	39.8	38.8	37.9	37.0	36.0	35.1
112	43.6	42.7	41.7	40.7	39.8	38.8	37.9	37.0	36.0	35.1
113	43.6	42.7	41.7	40.7	39.8	38.8	37.9	37.0	36.0	35.1
114	43.6	42.7	41.7	40.7	39.8	38.8	37.9	37.0	36.0	35.1
115+	43.6	42.7	41.7	40.7	39.8	38.8	37.9	37.0	36.0	35.1

Ages	50	51	52	53	54	55	56	57	58	59
	IRS Publication 590 Table II (continued)									
	(Joint Life and Last Survivor Expectancy)									
	(For Use by Owners Whose Spouses Are More Than 10 Years									
	Younger and Are the Sole Beneficiaries of Their IRAs)									
50	40.4	40.0	39.5	39.1	38.7	38.3	38.0	37.6	37.3	37.1
51	40.0	39.5	39.0	38.5	38.1	37.7	37.4	37.0	36.7	36.4
52	39.5	39.0	38.5	38.0	37.6	37.2	36.8	36.4	36.0	35.7
53	39.1	38.5	38.0	37.5	37.1	36.6	36.2	35.8	35.4	35.1
54	38.7	38.1	37.6	37.1	36.6	36.1	35.7	35.2	34.8	34.5
55	38.3	37.7	37.2	36.6	36.1	35.6	35.1	34.7	34.3	33.9
56	38.0	37.4	36.8	36.2	35.7	35.1	34.7	34.2	33.7	33.3
57	37.6	37.0	36.4	35.8	35.2	34.7	34.2	33.7	33.2	32.8
58	37.3	36.7	36.0	35.4	34.8	34.3	33.7	33.2	32.8	32.3
59	37.1	36.4	35.7	35.1	34.5	33.9	33.3	32.8	32.3	31.8
60	36.8	36.1	35.4	34.8	34.1	33.5	32.9	32.4	31.9	31.3
61	36.6	35.8	35.1	34.5	33.8	33.2	32.6	32.0	31.4	30.9
62	36.3	35.6	34.9	34.2	33.5	32.9	32.2	31.6	31.1	30.5
63	36.1	35.4	34.6	33.9	33.2	32.6	31.9	31.3	30.7	30.1
64	35.9	35.2	34.4	33.7	33.0	32.3	31.6	31.0	30.4	29.8
65	35.8	35.0	34.2	33.5	32.7	32.0	31.4	30.7	30.0	29.4
66	35.6	34.8	34.0	33.3	32.5	31.8	31.1	30.4	29.8	29.1
67	35.5	34.7	33.9	33.1	32.3	31.6	30.9	30.2	29.5	28.8
68	35.3	34.5	33.7	32.9	32.1	31.4	30.7	29.9	29.2	28.6
69	35.2	34.4	33.6	32.8	32.0	31.2	30.5	29.7	29.0	28.3
70	35.1	34.3	33.4	32.6	31.8	31.1	30.3	29.5	28.8	28.1
71	35.0	34.2	33.3	32.5	31.7	30.9	30.1	29.4	28.6	27.9
72	34.9	34.1	33.2	32.4	31.6	30.8	30.0	29.2	28.4	27.7
73	34.8	34.0	33.1	32.3	31.5	30.6	29.8	29.1	28.3	27.5
74	34.8	33.9	33.0	32.2	31.4	30.5	29.7	28.9	28.1	27.4
75	34.7	33.8	33.0	32.1	31.3	30.4	29.6	28.8	28.0	27.2

	IRS Publication 590 Table II (continued) (Joint Life and Last Survivor Expectancy) (For Use by Owners Whose Spouses Are More Than 10 Years Younger and Are the Sole Beneficiaries of Their IRAs)									
Ages	**50**	**51**	**52**	**53**	**54**	**55**	**56**	**57**	**58**	**59**
76	34.6	33.8	32.9	32.0	31.2	30.3	29.5	28.7	27.9	27.1
77	34.6	33.7	32.8	32.0	31.1	30.3	29.4	28.6	27.8	27.0
78	34.5	33.6	32.8	31.9	31.0	30.2	29.3	28.5	27.7	26.9
79	34.5	33.6	32.7	31.8	31.0	30.1	29.3	28.4	27.6	26.8
80	34.5	33.6	32.7	31.8	30.9	30.1	29.2	28.4	27.5	26.7
81	34.4	33.5	32.6	31.8	30.9	30.0	29.2	28.3	27.5	26.6
82	34.4	33.5	32.6	31.7	30.8	30.0	29.1	28.3	27.4	26.6
83	34.4	33.5	32.6	31.7	30.8	29.9	29.1	28.2	27.4	26.5
84	34.3	33.4	32.5	31.7	30.8	29.9	29.0	28.2	27.3	26.5
85	34.3	33.4	32.5	31.6	30.7	29.9	29.0	28.1	27.3	26.4
86	34.3	33.4	32.5	31.6	30.7	29.8	29.0	28.1	27.2	26.4
87	34.3	33.4	32.5	31.6	30.7	29.8	28.9	28.1	27.2	26.4
88	34.3	33.4	32.5	31.6	30.7	29.8	28.9	28.0	27.2	26.3
89	34.3	33.3	32.4	31.5	30.7	29.8	28.9	28.0	27.2	26.3
90	34.2	33.3	32.4	31.5	30.6	29.8	28.9	28.0	27.1	26.3
91	34.2	33.3	32.4	31.5	30.6	29.7	28.9	28.0	27.1	26.3
92	34.2	33.3	32.4	31.5	30.6	29.7	28.8	28.0	27.1	26.2
93	34.2	33.3	32.4	31.5	30.6	29.7	28.8	28.0	27.1	26.2
94	34.2	33.3	32.4	31.5	30.6	29.7	28.8	27.9	27.1	26.2
95	34.2	33.3	32.4	31.5	30.6	29.7	28.8	27.9	27.1	26.2
96	34.2	33.3	32.4	31.5	30.6	29.7	28.8	27.9	27.0	26.2
97	34.2	33.3	32.4	31.5	30.6	29.7	28.8	27.9	27.0	26.2
98	34.2	33.3	32.4	31.5	30.6	29.7	28.8	27.9	27.0	26.2
99	34.2	33.3	32.4	31.5	30.6	29.7	28.8	27.9	27.0	26.2
100	34.2	33.3	32.4	31.5	30.6	29.7	28.8	27.9	27.0	26.1
101	34.2	33.3	32.4	31.5	30.6	29.7	28.8	27.9	27.0	26.1

Ages	50	51	52	53	54	55	56	57	58	59
	IRS Publication 590 Table II (continued) (Joint Life and Last Survivor Expectancy) (For Use by Owners Whose Spouses Are More Than 10 Years Younger and Are the Sole Beneficiaries of Their IRAs)									
102	34.2	33.3	32.4	31.4	30.5	29.7	28.8	27.9	27.0	26.1
103	34.2	33.3	32.4	31.4	30.5	29.7	28.8	27.9	27.0	26.1
104	34.2	33.3	32.4	31.4	30.5	29.6	28.8	27.9	27.0	26.1
105	34.2	33.3	32.3	31.4	30.5	29.6	28.8	27.9	27.0	26.1
106	34.2	33.3	32.3	31.4	30.5	29.6	28.8	27.9	27.0	26.1
107	34.2	33.3	32.3	31.4	30.5	29.6	28.8	27.9	27.0	26.1
108	34.2	33.3	32.3	31.4	30.5	29.6	28.8	27.9	27.0	26.1
109	34.2	33.3	32.3	31.4	30.5	29.6	28.7	27.9	27.0	26.1
110	34.2	33.3	32.3	31.4	30.5	29.6	28.7	27.9	27.0	26.1
111	34.2	33.3	32.3	31.4	30.5	29.6	28.7	27.9	27.0	26.1
112	34.2	33.3	32.3	31.4	30.5	29.6	28.7	27.9	27.0	26.1
113	34.2	33.3	32.3	31.4	30.5	29.6	28.7	27.9	27.0	26.1
114	34.2	33.3	32.3	31.4	30.5	29.6	28.7	27.9	27.0	26.1
115+	34.2	33.3	32.3	31.4	30.5	29.6	28.7	27.9	27.0	26.1

Ages	60	61	62	63	64	65	66	67	68	69
60	30.9	30.4	30.0	29.6	29.2	28.8	28.5	28.2	27.9	27.6
61	30.4	29.9	29.5	29.0	28.6	28.3	27.9	27.6	27.3	27.0
62	30.0	29.5	29.0	28.5	28.1	27.7	27.3	27.0	26.7	26.4
63	29.6	29.0	28.5	28.1	27.6	27.2	26.8	26.4	26.1	25.7
64	29.2	28.6	28.1	27.6	27.1	26.7	26.3	25.9	25.5	25.2
65	28.8	28.3	27.7	27.2	26.7	26.2	25.8	25.4	25.0	24.6
66	28.5	27.9	27.3	26.8	26.3	25.8	25.3	24.9	24.5	24.1
67	28.2	27.6	27.0	26.4	25.9	25.4	24.9	24.4	24.0	23.6
68	27.9	27.3	26.7	26.1	25.5	25.0	24.5	24.0	23.5	23.1
69	27.6	27.0	26.4	25.7	25.2	24.6	24.1	23.6	23.1	22.6
70	27.4	26.7	26.1	25.4	24.8	24.3	23.7	23.2	22.7	22.2

IRS Publication 590 Table II (continued) (Joint Life and Last Survivor Expectancy) (For Use by Owners Whose Spouses Are More Than 10 Years Younger and Are the Sole Beneficiaries of Their IRAs)									
Ages	**60**	**61**	**62**	**63**	**64**	**65**	**66**	**67**	**68**	**69**
71	27.2	26.5	25.8	25.2	24.5	23.9	23.4	22.8	22.3	21.8
72	27.0	26.3	25.6	24.9	24.3	23.7	23.1	22.5	22.0	21.4
73	26.8	26.1	25.4	24.7	24.0	23.4	22.8	22.2	21.6	21.1
74	26.6	25.9	25.2	24.5	23.8	23.1	22.5	21.9	21.3	20.8
75	26.5	25.7	25.0	24.3	23.6	22.9	22.3	21.6	21.0	20.5
76	26.3	25.6	24.8	24.1	23.4	22.7	22.0	21.4	20.8	20.2
77	26.2	25.4	24.7	23.9	23.2	22.5	21.8	21.2	20.6	19.9
78	26.1	25.3	24.6	23.8	23.1	22.4	21.7	21.0	20.3	19.7
79	26.0	25.2	24.4	23.7	22.9	22.2	21.5	20.8	20.1	19.5
80	25.9	25.1	24.3	23.6	22.8	22.1	21.3	20.6	20.0	19.3
81	25.8	25.0	24.2	23.4	22.7	21.9	21.2	20.5	19.8	19.1
82	25.8	24.9	24.1	23.4	22.6	21.8	21.1	20.4	19.7	19.0
83	25.7	24.9	24.1	23.3	22.5	21.7	21.0	20.2	19.5	18.8
84	25.6	24.8	24.0	23.2	22.4	21.6	20.9	20.1	19.4	18.7
85	25.6	24.8	23.9	23.1	22.3	21.6	20.8	20.1	19.3	18.6
86	25.5	24.7	23.9	23.1	22.3	21.5	20.7	20.0	19.2	18.5
87	25.5	24.7	23.8	23.0	22.2	21.4	20.7	19.9	19.2	18.4
88	25.5	24.6	23.8	23.0	22.2	21.4	20.6	19.8	19.1	18.3
89	25.4	24.6	23.8	22.9	22.1	21.3	20.5	19.8	19.0	18.3
90	25.4	24.6	23.7	22.9	22.1	21.3	20.5	19.7	19.0	18.2
91	25.4	24.5	23.7	22.9	22.1	21.3	20.5	19.7	18.9	18.2
92	25.4	24.5	23.7	22.9	22.0	21.2	20.4	19.6	18.9	18.1
93	25.4	24.5	23.7	22.8	22.0	21.2	20.4	19.6	18.8	18.1
94	25.3	24.5	23.6	22.8	22.0	21.2	20.4	19.6	18.8	18.0
95	25.3	24.5	23.6	22.8	22.0	21.1	20.3	19.6	18.8	18.0
96	25.3	24.5	23.6	22.8	21.9	21.1	20.3	19.5	18.8	18.0

IRS Publication 590 Table II (continued) (Joint Life and Last Survivor Expectancy) (For Use by Owners Whose Spouses Are More Than 10 Years Younger and Are the Sole Beneficiaries of Their IRAs)									
Ages	**60**	**61**	**62**	**63**	**64**	**65**	**66**	**67**	**68**	**69**
97	25.3	24.5	23.6	22.8	21.9	21.1	20.3	19.5	18.7	18.0
98	25.3	24.4	23.6	22.8	21.9	21.1	20.3	19.5	18.7	17.9
99	25.3	24.4	23.6	22.7	21.9	21.1	20.3	19.5	18.7	17.9
100	25.3	24.4	23.6	22.7	21.9	21.1	20.3	19.5	18.7	17.9
101	25.3	24.4	23.6	22.7	21.9	21.1	20.2	19.4	18.7	17.9
102	25.3	24.4	23.6	22.7	21.9	21.1	20.2	19.4	18.6	17.9
103	25.3	24.4	23.6	22.7	21.9	21.0	20.2	19.4	18.6	17.9
104	25.3	24.4	23.5	22.7	21.9	21.0	20.2	19.4	18.6	17.8
105	25.3	24.4	23.5	22.7	21.9	21.0	20.2	19.4	18.6	17.8
106	25.3	24.4	23.5	22.7	21.9	21.0	20.2	19.4	18.6	17.8
107	25.2	24.4	23.5	22.7	21.8	21.0	20.2	19.4	18.6	17.8
108	25.2	24.4	23.5	22.7	21.8	21.0	20.2	19.4	18.6	17.8
109	25.2	24.4	23.5	22.7	21.8	21.0	20.2	19.4	18.6	17.8
110	25.2	24.4	23.5	22.7	21.8	21.0	20.2	19.4	18.6	17.8
111	25.2	24.4	23.5	22.7	21.8	21.0	20.2	19.4	18.6	17.8
112	25.2	24.4	23.5	22.7	21.8	21.0	20.2	19.4	18.6	17.8
113	25.2	24.4	23.5	22.7	21.8	21.0	20.2	19.4	18.6	17.8
114	25.2	24.4	23.5	22.7	21.8	21.0	20.2	19.4	18.6	17.8
115+	25.2	24.4	23.5	22.7	21.8	21.0	20.2	19.4	18.6	17.8
Ages	**70**	**71**	**72**	**73**	**74**	**75**	**76**	**77**	**78**	**79**
70	21.8	21.3	20.9	20.6	20.2	19.9	19.6	19.4	19.1	18.9
71	21.3	20.9	20.5	20.1	19.7	19.4	19.1	18.8	18.5	18.3
72	20.9	20.5	20.0	19.6	19.3	18.9	18.6	18.3	18.0	17.7
73	20.6	20.1	19.6	19.2	18.8	18.4	18.1	17.8	17.5	17.2
74	20.2	19.7	19.3	18.8	18.4	18.0	17.6	17.3	17.0	16.7
75	19.9	19.4	18.9	18.4	18.0	17.6	17.2	16.8	16.5	16.2

Ages	70	71	72	73	74	75	76	77	78	79
IRS Publication 590 Table II (continued)										
(Joint Life and Last Survivor Expectancy)										
(For Use by Owners Whose Spouses Are More Than 10 Years Younger and Are the Sole Beneficiaries of Their IRAs)										
76	19.6	19.1	18.6	18.1	17.6	17.2	16.8	16.4	16.0	15.7
77	19.4	18.8	18.3	17.8	17.3	16.8	16.4	16.0	15.6	15.3
78	19.1	18.5	18.0	17.5	17.0	16.5	16.0	15.6	15.2	14.9
79	18.9	18.3	17.7	17.2	16.7	16.2	15.7	15.3	14.9	14.5
80	18.7	18.1	17.5	16.9	16.4	15.9	15.4	15.0	14.5	14.1
81	18.5	17.9	17.3	16.7	16.2	15.6	15.1	14.7	14.2	13.8
82	18.3	17.7	17.1	16.5	15.9	15.4	14.9	14.4	13.9	13.5
83	18.2	17.5	16.9	16.3	15.7	15.2	14.7	14.2	13.7	13.2
84	18.0	17.4	16.7	16.1	15.5	15.0	14.4	13.9	13.4	13.0
85	17.9	17.3	16.6	16.0	15.4	14.8	14.3	13.7	13.2	12.8
86	17.8	17.1	16.5	15.8	15.2	14.6	14.1	13.5	13.0	12.5
87	17.7	17.0	16.4	15.7	15.1	14.5	13.9	13.4	12.9	12.4
88	17.6	16.9	16.3	15.6	15.0	14.4	13.8	13.2	12.7	12.2
89	17.6	16.9	16.2	15.5	14.9	14.3	13.7	13.1	12.6	12.0
90	17.5	16.8	16.1	15.4	14.8	14.2	13.6	13.0	12.4	11.9
91	17.4	16.7	16.0	15.4	14.7	14.1	13.5	12.9	12.3	11.8
92	17.4	16.7	16.0	15.3	14.6	14.0	13.4	12.8	12.2	11.7
93	17.3	16.6	15.9	15.2	14.6	13.9	13.3	12.7	12.1	11.6
94	17.3	16.6	15.9	15.2	14.5	13.9	13.2	12.6	12.0	11.5
95	17.3	16.5	15.8	15.1	14.5	13.8	13.2	12.6	12.0	11.4
96	17.2	16.5	15.8	15.1	14.4	13.8	13.1	12.5	11.9	11.3
97	17.2	16.5	15.8	15.1	14.4	13.7	13.1	12.5	11.9	11.3
98	17.2	16.4	15.7	15.0	14.3	13.7	13.0	12.4	11.8	11.2
99	17.2	16.4	15.7	15.0	14.3	13.6	13.0	12.4	11.8	11.2
100	17.1	16.4	15.7	15.0	14.3	13.6	12.9	12.3	11.7	11.1
101	17.1	16.4	15.6	14.9	14.2	13.6	12.9	12.3	11.7	11.1

Ages	70	71	72	73	74	75	76	77	78	79
102	17.1	16.4	15.6	14.9	14.2	13.5	12.9	12.2	11.6	11.0
103	17.1	16.3	15.6	14.9	14.2	13.5	12.9	12.2	11.6	11.0
104	17.1	16.3	15.6	14.9	14.2	13.5	12.8	12.2	11.6	11.0
105	17.1	16.3	15.6	14.9	14.2	13.5	12.8	12.2	11.5	10.9
106	17.1	16.3	15.6	14.8	14.1	13.5	12.8	12.2	11.5	10.9
107	17.0	16.3	15.6	14.8	14.1	13.4	12.8	12.1	11.5	10.9
108	17.0	16.3	15.5	14.8	14.1	13.4	12.8	12.1	11.5	10.9
109	17.0	16.3	15.5	14.8	14.1	13.4	12.8	12.1	11.5	10.9
110	17.0	16.3	15.5	14.8	14.1	13.4	12.7	12.1	11.5	10.9
111	17.0	16.3	15.5	14.8	14.1	13.4	12.7	12.1	11.5	10.8
112	17.0	16.3	15.5	14.8	14.1	13.4	12.7	12.1	11.5	10.8
113	17.0	16.3	15.5	14.8	14.1	13.4	12.7	12.1	11.4	10.8
114	17.0	16.3	15.5	14.8	14.1	13.4	12.7	12.1	11.4	10.8
115+	17.0	16.3	15.5	14.8	14.1	13.4	12.7	12.1	11.4	10.8
Ages	80	81	82	83	84	85	86	87	88	89
80	13.8	13.4	13.1	12.8	12.6	12.3	12.1	11.9	11.7	11.5
81	13.4	13.1	12.7	12.4	12.2	11.9	11.7	11.4	11.3	11.1
82	13.1	12.7	12.4	12.1	11.8	11.5	11.3	11.0	10.8	10.6
83	12.8	12.4	12.1	11.7	11.4	11.1	10.9	10.6	10.4	10.2
84	12.6	12.2	11.8	11.4	11.1	10.8	10.5	10.3	10.1	9.9
85	12.3	11.9	11.5	11.1	10.8	10.5	10.2	9.9	9.7	9.5
86	12.1	11.7	11.3	10.9	10.5	10.2	9.9	9.6	9.4	9.2
87	11.9	11.4	11.0	10.6	10.3	9.9	9.6	9.4	9.1	8.9
88	11.7	11.3	10.8	10.4	10.1	9.7	9.4	9.1	8.8	8.6
89	11.5	11.1	10.6	10.2	9.9	9.5	9.2	8.9	8.6	8.3
90	11.4	10.9	10.5	10.1	9.7	9.3	9.0	8.6	8.3	8.1

IRS Publication 590 Table II (continued) (Joint Life and Last Survivor Expectancy) (For Use by Owners Whose Spouses Are More Than 10 Years Younger and Are the Sole Beneficiaries of Their IRAs)

Ages	80	81	82	83	84	85	86	87	88	89

IRS Publication 590 Table II (continued)
(Joint Life and Last Survivor Expectancy)
(For Use by Owners Whose Spouses Are More Than 10 Years Younger and Are the Sole Beneficiaries of Their IRAs)

Ages	80	81	82	83	84	85	86	87	88	89
91	11.3	10.8	10.3	9.9	9.5	9.1	8.8	8.4	8.1	7.9
92	11.2	10.7	10.2	9.8	9.3	9.0	8.6	8.3	8.0	7.7
93	11.1	10.6	10.1	9.6	9.2	8.8	8.5	8.1	7.8	7.5
94	11.0	10.5	10.0	9.5	9.1	8.7	8.3	8.0	7.6	7.3
95	10.9	10.4	9.9	9.4	9.0	8.6	8.2	7.8	7.5	7.2
96	10.8	10.3	9.8	9.3	8.9	8.5	8.1	7.7	7.4	7.1
97	10.7	10.2	9.7	9.2	8.8	8.4	8.0	7.6	7.3	6.9
98	10.7	10.1	9.6	9.2	8.7	8.3	7.9	7.5	7.1	6.8
99	10.6	10.1	9.6	9.1	8.6	8.2	7.8	7.4	7.0	6.7
100	10.6	10.0	9.5	9.0	8.5	8.1	7.7	7.3	6.9	6.6
101	10.5	10.0	9.4	9.0	8.5	8.0	7.6	7.2	6.9	6.5
102	10.5	9.9	9.4	8.9	8.4	8.0	7.5	7.1	6.8	6.4
103	10.4	9.9	9.4	8.8	8.4	7.9	7.5	7.1	6.7	6.3
104	10.4	9.8	9.3	8.8	8.3	7.9	7.4	7.0	6.6	6.3
105	10.4	9.8	9.3	8.8	8.3	7.8	7.4	7.0	6.6	6.2
106	10.3	9.8	9.2	8.7	8.2	7.8	7.3	6.9	6.5	6.2
107	10.3	9.8	9.2	8.7	8.2	7.7	7.3	6.9	6.5	6.1
108	10.3	9.7	9.2	8.7	8.2	7.7	7.3	6.8	6.4	6.1
109	10.3	9.7	9.2	8.7	8.2	7.7	7.2	6.8	6.4	6.0
110	10.3	9.7	9.2	8.6	8.1	7.7	7.2	6.8	6.4	6.0
111	10.3	9.7	9.1	8.6	8.1	7.6	7.2	6.8	6.3	6.0
112	10.2	9.7	9.1	8.6	8.1	7.6	7.2	6.7	6.3	5.9
113	10.2	9.7	9.1	8.6	8.1	7.6	7.2	6.7	6.3	5.9
114	10.2	9.7	9.1	8.6	8.1	7.6	7.1	6.7	6.3	5.9
115+	10.2	9.7	9.1	8.6	8.1	7.6	7.1	6.7	6.3	5.9

Ages	90	91	92	93	94	95	96	97	98	99

IRS Publication 590 Table II (continued)
(Joint Life and Last Survivor Expectancy)
(For Use by Owners Whose Spouses Are More Than 10 Years Younger and Are the Sole Beneficiaries of Their IRAs)

Ages	90	91	92	93	94	95	96	97	98	99
90	7.8	7.6	7.4	7.2	7.1	6.9	6.8	6.6	6.5	6.4
91	7.6	7.4	7.2	7.0	6.8	6.7	6.5	6.4	6.3	6.1
92	7.4	7.2	7.0	6.8	6.6	6.4	6.3	6.1	6.0	5.9
93	7.2	7.0	6.8	6.6	6.4	6.2	6.1	5.9	5.8	5.6
94	7.1	6.8	6.6	6.4	6.2	6.0	5.9	5.7	5.6	5.4
95	6.9	6.7	6.4	6.2	6.0	5.8	5.7	5.5	5.4	5.2
96	6.8	6.5	6.3	6.1	5.9	5.7	5.5	5.3	5.2	5.0
97	6.6	6.4	6.1	5.9	5.7	5.5	5.3	5.2	5.0	4.9
98	6.5	6.3	6.0	5.8	5.6	5.4	5.2	5.0	4.8	4.7
99	6.4	6.1	5.9	5.6	5.4	5.2	5.0	4.9	4.7	4.5
100	6.3	6.0	5.8	5.5	5.3	5.1	4.9	4.7	4.5	4.4
101	6.2	5.9	5.6	5.4	5.2	5.0	4.8	4.6	4.4	4.2
102	6.1	5.8	5.5	5.3	5.1	4.8	4.6	4.4	4.3	4.1
103	6.0	5.7	5.4	5.2	5.0	4.7	4.5	4.3	4.1	4.0
104	5.9	5.6	5.4	5.1	4.9	4.6	4.4	4.2	4.0	3.8
105	5.9	5.6	5.3	5.0	4.8	4.5	4.3	4.1	3.9	3.7
106	5.8	5.5	5.2	4.9	4.7	4.5	4.2	4.0	3.8	3.6
107	5.8	5.4	5.1	4.9	4.6	4.4	4.2	3.9	3.7	3.5
108	5.7	5.4	5.1	4.8	4.6	4.3	4.1	3.9	3.7	3.5
109	5.7	5.3	5.0	4.8	4.5	4.3	4.0	3.8	3.6	3.4
110	5.6	5.3	5.0	4.7	4.5	4.2	4.0	3.8	3.5	3.3
111	5.6	5.3	5.0	4.7	4.4	4.2	3.9	3.7	3.5	3.3
112	5.6	5.3	4.9	4.7	4.4	4.1	3.9	3.7	3.5	3.2
113	5.6	5.2	4.9	4.6	4.4	4.1	3.9	3.6	3.4	3.2
114	5.6	5.2	4.9	4.6	4.3	4.1	3.9	3.6	3.4	3.2
115+	5.5	5.2	4.9	4.6	4.3	4.1	3.8	3.6	3.4	3.1

IRS Publication 590 Table II (continued) (Joint Life and Last Survivor Expectancy) (For Use by Owners Whose Spouses Are More Than 10 Years Younger and Are the Sole Beneficiaries of Their IRAs)									
Ages	**100**	**101**	**102**	**103**	**104**	**105**	**106**	**107**	**108**	**109**
100	4.2	4.1	3.9	3.8	3.7	3.5	3.4	3.3	3.3	3.2
101	4.1	3.9	3.7	3.6	3.5	3.4	3.2	3.1	3.1	3.0
102	3.9	3.7	3.6	3.4	3.3	3.2	3.1	3.0	2.9	2.8
103	3.8	3.6	3.4	3.3	3.2	3.0	2.9	2.8	2.7	2.6
104	3.7	3.5	3.3	3.2	3.0	2.9	2.7	2.6	2.5	2.4
105	3.5	3.4	3.2	3.0	2.9	2.7	2.6	2.5	2.4	2.3
106	3.4	3.2	3.1	2.9	2.7	2.6	2.4	2.3	2.2	2.1
107	3.3	3.1	3.0	2.8	2.6	2.5	2.3	2.2	2.1	2.0
108	3.3	3.1	2.9	2.7	2.5	2.4	2.2	2.1	1.9	1.8
109	3.2	3.0	2.8	2.6	2.4	2.3	2.1	2.0	1.8	1.7
110	3.1	2.9	2.7	2.5	2.3	2.2	2.0	1.9	1.7	1.6
111	3.1	2.9	2.7	2.5	2.3	2.1	1.9	1.8	1.6	1.5
112	3.0	2.8	2.6	2.4	2.2	2.0	1.9	1.7	1.5	1.4
113	3.0	2.8	2.6	2.4	2.2	2.0	1.8	1.6	1.5	1.3
114	3.0	2.7	2.5	2.3	2.1	1.9	1.8	1.6	1.4	1.3
115+	2.9	2.7	2.5	2.3	2.1	1.9	1.7	1.5	1.4	1.2
Ages	**110**	**111**	**112**	**113**	**114**	**115+**				
110	1.5	1.4	1.3	1.2	1.1	1.1				
111	1.4	1.2	1.1	1.1	1.0	1.0				
112	1.3	1.1	1.0	1.0	1.0	1.0				
113	1.2	1.1	1.0	1.0	1.0	1.0				
114	1.1	1.0	1.0	1.0	1.0	1.0				
115+	1.1	1.0	1.0	1.0	1.0	1.0				

www.ingramcontent.com/pod-product-compliance
Lightning Source LLC
Chambersburg PA
CBHW070403200326
41518CB00011B/2039